D1486251

04218186

The Flying Scotsman Story

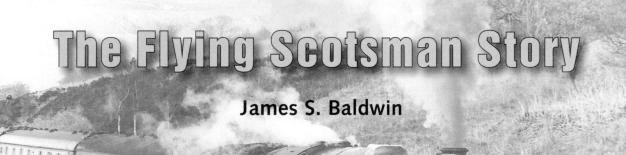

The Flying Scotsman Story

James S. Baldwin

The
HISTORY
Press

Published in the United Kingdom in 2014 by
The History Press
The Mill · Brimscombe Port · Stroud · Gloucestershire · GL5 2QG

British Library Cataloguing in Publication Data
A catalogue record for this book is available from the British
Library.

Hardback ISBN 978-0-7524-9452-4

Typesetting and origination by The History Press
Printed in India

Cover illustrations.
Front: No.4472 *Flying Scotsman* worked a round trip tour on
3 June 1989 from Sydney to Moss Vale in Australia. It proceeded
east to Unanderra and returned north to Sydney along to South
Coast Line. (Rob Turner)
Back: No.60103 *Flying Scotsman* at Doncaster Carr locomotive
depot, 1958. (Author's Collection)

CONTENTS

Almost everyone is aware of the *Flying Scotsman*, but what is it?

First, there is the 4-6-2 – or as this type of wheel arrangement is generally known, Pacific – type of steam locomotive that was designed by Herbert Nigel Gresley and built at Doncaster Works. Costing £7,944 to construct, it was part of a new generation of motive power needed on the East Coast Main Line to satisfy the ever-increasing volume of passenger traffic between London and Edinburgh.

Did You Know?
Flying Scotsman is capable of hauling a load of 600 tons and consumes 45lb of coal and 40 gallons of water each mile.

◀ No.4472 *Flying Scotsman* is seen with the eponymous train on 7 July 1934. (W.B. Greenfield, courtesy of the NELPG)

▽ On 13 November 1965, No.4472 *Flying Scotsman* broke the record for the fastest run ever for a steam locomotive from Paddington to Cardiff, working the 'Panda Pullman' fundraising special. On the return run it also broke the steam record for the fastest run ever for a steam locomotive between Cardiff and Paddington. (D. Trevor Rowe)

It was No.4472 *Flying Scotsman* that worked the first non-stop 'Flying Scotsman' service from King's Cross to Edinburgh in 1928, and in 1929 it starred in the UK's first 'talkie' movie – *The Flying Scotsman*.

Over the following years *Flying Scotsman* made many public appearances and performances, creating a worldwide public awareness, the result of which was that the loco became known as 'the most famous steam locomotive in the world'!

Now we turn to the second Flying Scotsman – the 'Flying Scotsman' train which still runs between London and Edinburgh.

 No.4472 *Flying Scotsman* and its exhibition train are seen winding their way on the early stages of their North America tour in 1969. (The Southern Museum of Civil War & Locomotive History, Kennesaw, Georgia Collection)

No.4472 *Flying Scotsman* is seen at Pier 41 on the Embarcadero in San Francisco, with part of the exhibition train seen on the left. The sailing ship is the *Balclutha*, built in 1886, which is the only steel-hulled full-rigged sailing ship left in the San Francisco Bay area. Alan Miller, a friend of the photographer, dated the image to 18 March 1972. (Jack Neville)

A close-up of one of the cab-side mounted LNER coats of arms that were carried by No.4472 *Flying Scotsman* during its North American tour. The author is the proud owner of the crest that was carried on the fireman's side and Sir William McAlpine owns the other. (Jack Neville)

⬆ On 12 August 1972, No.4472 *Flying Scotsman* and its train were ferried back to Oakland from San Francisco on the ferry *Las Plumas*. Hauled behind Western Pacific U-23B class diesel-electric locomotive No.2260, they passed through the slums of Oakland eastwards to Stockton, where the ensemble is seen having arrived mid-afternoon at Sharp Army Depot in Lathrop and were placed in secure storage. (Jack Neville)

◀ No.4472 *Flying Scotsman* is seen at Market Overton, where it was moved for a short stay during 1974 by its then owner Sir William McAlpine. (Sir William McAlpine Collection)

The author is seen filming and interviewing Roland Kennington, the chief engineer of *Flying Scotsman*, in the NRM's yard at York soon after *Flying Scotsman* had successfully completed the Inaugural Scotsman run on 4 July 1999. (Grahame Plater)

over the years, without ever establishing an identity.

Then, at 10:00 on 1 May 1928, the locomotive *Flying Scotsman* worked the first regular non-stop 'Flying Scotsman' service from King's Cross to Edinburgh Waverley and the train was renamed. The legendary 'Flying Scotsman' had officially arrived.

So there are in fact two Flying Scotsmans, and yes, they are connected!

This prestigious and long-standing express passenger train service from the GNR's King's Cross Station, London and the NBR's Waverley Station, Edinburgh had been popular since June 1862. This train had been known by a variety of names

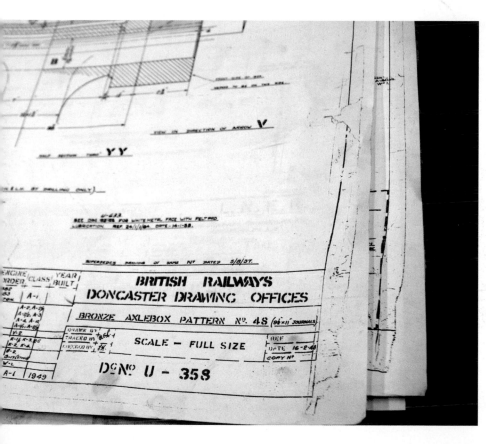

◄◄◄ By the end of March 2012, work was completed on the designing, manufacturing and riveting of the new mid-stretcher for *Flying Scotsman*'s frames at Riley & Son (E) Ltd. (Author)

◄ Here is a full-size drawing, numbered U-358, produced by British Railways' Doncaster Drawing Office, showing the details of a Bronze Axlebox Pattern, as was used by engineers at Riley & Son (E) Ltd during the repair work being carried out to *Flying Scotsman* during the spring of 2012. Note that the locomotive class is put as 'A1' and the year of manufacture as '1949'. *Flying Scotsman* was converted to A3 class in January 1947, with No.60068 *Sir Visto* being the last A1 locomotive to be converted, in December 1948. (Author)

▲ *Tornado* was completed in 2008 at Darlington, England. It was the first main-line standard gauge steam locomotive to be built in the UK since *Evening Star* in 1960. As another contender for the title of 'The Most Famous Steam Locomotive in the World', it is seen in BR 'blue' livery as it 'attacks' Grosvenor Bank on 29 November 2012, working the Cathedrals Express charter from Victoria Station, London, to Bristol. *Tornado* was built to a design which is a derivative of *Flying Scotsman*. (Author)

▼ On 27 May 2011 *Flying Scotsman* was unveiled to an invited audience after its prolonged overhaul at the NRM, York. It is seen in wartime black livery just after the unveiling ceremony and has the number 103 painted on the driver's cab side, with the number 502 painted on the fireman's cab side and the front buffer beam. Time would show that the overhaul of *Flying Scotsman* was in fact far from over, with the revelation of cracks in the frames being discovered and that it would need to be stripped down again to inspect the middle cylinder. (Author)

▲ Built at Springburn Works, Glasgow, in 1886, Caledonian Railway 4-4-0 No.123's greatest claim to fame is its participation in the celebrated Race to the North, which took place between East Coast & West Coast railway companies in 1888. After a working life of almost fifty years, No.123 was stored away until the late 1950s, when BR staff decided to restore No.123 to its former glory. In September 2010, it was moved to the new Riverside Museum in Glasgow for display. (Author's Collection)

The East Coast Main Line over which the 'Flying Scotsman' service runs was built in the nineteenth century by many small railway companies. Mergers and acquisitions led to three main companies controlling the route: the Great Northern Railway (GNR), the North British Railway (NBR) and the North Eastern Railway (NER).

As we have seen, regular fast passenger services between England and Scotland began in 1862. The journey took 10½ hours to complete and included a 30-minute stop at York for lunch. But passengers suffered badly as they tried in vain to consume their scalding hot soup in a rush, in almost circus-like conditions. Rail passenger growth increased competition in rail travel, as did improvements in technology.

Introduced in 1870 was a locomotive with 8ft 1in driving wheels, designed by Patrick Stirling specifically for high-speed express services between York and London. The norm in those days was to use inside cylinders; however, there were frequent failures. The cranked axle shafts could not cope with such large drivers and the boilers would have been set too high. Patrick Stirling therefore used outside cylinders with a four-wheeled bogie at the front end for lateral stability. These locomotives' single pair of large driving wheels led to their nickname of 'eight-footers' and they were originally designed to haul up to twenty-six passenger carriages at an average speed of 47mph. A total of fifty-three examples were built at Doncaster Works between 1870 and 1895.

Then, over two summers in the late nineteenth century, British passenger trains literally raced each other from London to Scotland over the two principal routes – the East Coast Main Line and the West

◅ The Great Northern Railway's small boiler C2 class locomotive was the first 4-4-2 or Atlantic-type locomotive to be introduced in Great Britain and was designed by Henry Ivatt. Twenty-two members of the class were built between 1898 and 1903 at Doncaster Works. The class were commonly known as 'Klondikes', after the 1897 Klondike gold rush. (Author's Collection)

Great Northern Express

◅ With the arrival of the Ivatt Atlantic class locomotives after 1898, the class of Stirling's Single locomotives began to be displaced from the most prestigious express services. The first of the class, No.1, is preserved at the National Railway Museum, York. Here we see Stirling Single No.774 piloting a Stirling-designed 2-2-2 locomotive on a GNR Express working. (Author's Collection)

The diagram shows the boiler arrangements for the original A1 class Pacific, after it had been reclassified as an A10 class, and the subsequent A3 class with a higher boiler pressure. Both A1 and A3 boilers had the round dome fitted originally as is shown here. *Flying Scotsman* was the third A1 class Pacific to be constructed with this type of boiler, known as a 'Boiler No.94'. (Peter Townend Collection)

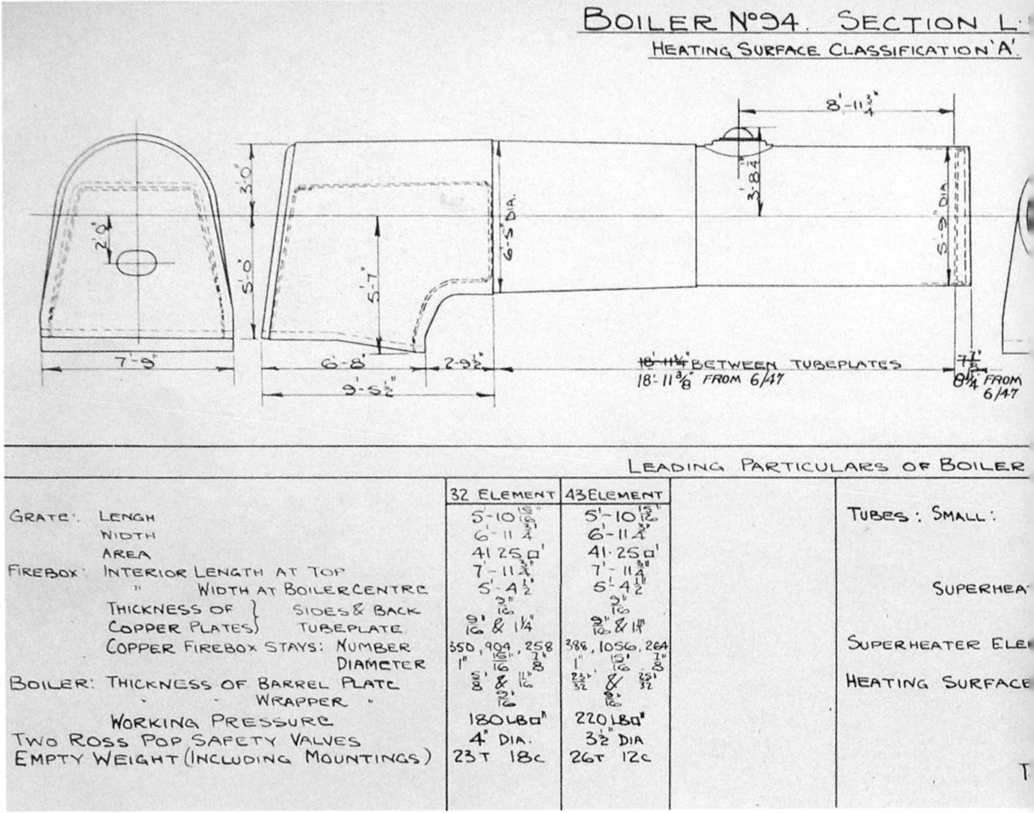

BOILER Nº94. SECTION L
HEATING SURFACE CLASSIFICATION 'A'.
8'-11 3/4"
3'-0"
2'-0"
5'-0"
5'-7"
6'-5" DIA.
3'-8 1/4"
5'-9" DIA.
7'-9"
6'-8"
2'-9 1/2"
9'-5 1/2"
18'-11 1/4" BETWEEN TUBEPLATES
18'-11 3/8" FROM 6/47
7 7/8"
8 1/4" FROM 6/47
LEADING PARTICULARS OF BOILER
TUBES: SMALL:
SUPERHEA
SUPERHEATER ELE
HEATING SURFACE

	32 ELEMENT	43 ELEMENT
GRATE: LENGH	5'-10 15/16"	5'-10 15/16"
WIDTH	6'-11 3/4"	6'-11 3/4"
AREA	41 25 □'	41·25 □'
FIREBOX: INTERIOR LENGTH AT TOP	7'-11 3/4"	7'-11 3/4"
" WIDTH AT BOILER CENTRE	5'-4 1/2"	5'-4 1/2"
THICKNESS OF COPPER PLATES: SIDES & BACK	9/16"	9/16"
TUBEPLATE	9/16" & 1 1/4"	9/16" & 1 1/4"
COPPER FIREBOX STAYS: NUMBER	350, 904, 258	388, 1056, 264
DIAMETER	1", 15/16", 7/8"	1", 15/16", 7/8"
BOILER: THICKNESS OF BARREL PLATE	5/8" & 11/16"	23/32" & 25/32"
" " WRAPPER "	9/16"	9/16"
WORKING PRESSURE	180 LB □"	220 LB □"
TWO ROSS POP SAFETY VALVES	4" DIA.	3 1/2" DIA
EMPTY WEIGHT (INCLUDING MOUNTINGS)	23 T 18 C	26 T 12 C

TYPE	NUMBER OF ENGINES.
A-10.	
A-3.	
~~BT~~	

THIS NUMBER INCLUDES:–

SEE ALSO 94A

	32 ELEMENT	43 ELEMENT
~ERIAL	STEEL	STEEL
~MBER	168	121
OUTSIDE	2¼"	2¼"
~ICKNESS	10 WG	10 WG
~MBER	32	43
~A. OUTSIDE	5¼"	5¼"
~ICKNESS	5/32	5/32
~MBER	32	43
~A. INSIDE	1.244"	1.244"
~REBOX	215 ☐'	215 ☐'
~BES 2¼"	1880 ·	1354.2 ☐'
~UES 5¼	835 "	1122.8 ☐'
~APORATIVE	2930 ·	2692.0 "
~EMENTS	525 "	706.0 "
~NG SURFACE	3455 ☐'	3398 ☐'

▲ In December 1902, the first of H.A. Ivatt's large Atlantic-type locomotives – No.251 – entered service in Great Britain. Developed as an enlarged version of the Klondike type, it was built as a more powerful, free-steaming locomotive, which was required to work the fastest and heaviest express passenger trains on the GNR. With a boiler diameter increased from 4ft 8in to 5ft 6in, these large-boilered Atlantics became the first locomotives to be built with a wide firebox and were seen as the start of the East Coast Main Line's 'Big Engine' policy. (Author's Collection)

Coast Main Line. The rivalry for supremacy became known as 'the Race to the North'. The outcome was that the overall time from London to Edinburgh was reduced during 1888 to 8½ hours: an improvement of two hours.

After the 'Railway Races' of 1888 and 1895, the high speeds attained on the 'Scotch Expresses' were limited by mutual agreement between the competing railway companies.

So with the ever growing pressure of improved timings and greater loadings on the 'Scotch Expresses', the GNR was seeking to lead the market and introduced the first

During March 1924, No.4472 *Flying Scotsman* was repainted in the paint shop at Doncaster Works prior to being covered in a bespoke dust sheet in preparation to being put on display to the public in the 'Palace of Engineering', Wembley. This is what *Flying Scotsman* looked like for the open day held for the plant employees and their families. Admission was 6*d* and the proceeds went to the Doncaster Infirmary. The very high standard of workmanship in preparing it to exhibition standards is clearly seen in this image. (Sir William McAlpine Collection)

No.4472 *Flying Scotsman* is seen coupled to corridor tender No.5323, which had replaced its original tender, No.5223, from 16 November 1925 until 14 February 1928. The detail of the tender is seen to good effect as *Flying Scotsman* is turned on the King's Cross turntable. (Author's Collection)

Did You Know?

H.N. Gresley lived at Salisbury Hall, near St Albans in Hertfordshire. In the moat around his home, Gresley developed an interest in breeding wild birds and ducks – some of which were mallards. Perhaps they inspired the naming of the most famous of Gresley's later A4 class? The hall still exists today as the home of the de Havilland Aircraft Heritage Centre.

➤ This is an official photograph taken for publicity purposes for the LNER to promote their new 'corridor tender' for the non-stop 'Flying Scotsman' service from King's Cross to Edinburgh Waverley. A clean and fresh driver is seen entering the cab via the tender's corridor. At the top of the picture are the neatly put away fire-irons, but in reality they were usually stored on the floor of the tender's corridor. The larger of the two controls was the handbrake and the smaller one regulated the flow of water from the tender to the ejectors. To the left of the driver's hand is written '2-4-28', which is the paint date of the tender. Three days later, on 5 April 1928, No.4472 *Flying Scotsman* left Doncaster Works after a general repair, during which it had been coupled to corridor tender No.5323, as seen here. (Author's Collection)

4-4-2 or Atlantic type of locomotive into Great Britain. Designed by Henry Ivatt in 1897 and built at Doncaster Works, the class were commonly known as 'Klondikes' after the 1897 Klondike gold rush.

Atlantics, with their larger boilers, were then introduced, improving the service yet again, but when H.N. Gresley succeeded Henry Ivatt in 1911, Gresley was under pressure to do something special.

He looked around for new ideas and his attention was drawn Stateside, where he become inspired by the Pennsylvania Railroad's K4s class steam locomotive – a true American classic. The K4s class first ran in 1914 and was soon a familiar sight as it became the Pennsylvania Railroad's premiere steam passenger locomotive, with 425 examples built.

Inspired by the K4s class, but using many of his own designs, H.N. Gresley produced the first of two examples of

his three-cylinder express passenger Pacific locomotives – No.1470, which was put to work on the GNR in 1922. It soon proved itself to be satisfactory, with an order placed for a further ten locomotives to be constructed.

The third member of the class to be completed was in fact the first of the second

▲ No.4472 *Flying Scotsman* is seen preparing to depart from Newcastle Station with a passenger service on 1 August 1934. Notice that the water crane is positioned over the tender. (W.B. Greenfield, courtesy of the NELPG)

batch to be ordered and, when delivered in 1923, it became the first express passenger locomotive to be officially delivered to the newly formed London and North Eastern Railway (despite having been ordered during the days of the GNR in 1922). It was given the number 1472, but in a short time this locomotive would be renumbered, given a very special name, and would become the world famous No.4472 *Flying Scotsman*.

Before road and air transport became common, the East Coast Main Line services had longer through routes and were becoming ever heavier and quicker. They therefore required very powerful locomotives to operate these services. No.4472 *Flying Scotsman* was part of a class of locomotives that were specifically designed to work these increasingly heavy and faster services.

Herbert Nigel Gresley was born in Edinburgh in June 1876 and was educated at Marlborough College. His railway career began at Crewe as a pupil of the London and North Western Railway (or LNWR), where a system of using components machined to such fine tolerances so as to make them interchangeable was commonplace, as was the split cast-iron piston ring, which is still in use in every piston engine throughout the world today. In 1860, the use of the water trough was developed here, enabling locomotives to work on long runs without stopping. This system would be used by Gresley on his famous non-stop runs from London to Edinburgh.

At the LNWR the Teutonic class loco-motive had 3-cylinders, three sets of valve gear and a 2-2-2-0 wheel arrangement, which suffered problems in starting as the driving wheels, which were not coupled together, would sometimes oppose each other when starting. H.N. Gresley's awareness of these complex problems would have put him off the idea of using such a mechanism in his designs. However, they 'focused the mind' and inspired him to use the much simpler 2 to 1 lever mechanism on his future Pacific locomotives.

In 1898 he moved on to study at the Lancashire and Yorkshire Railway's Horwich works and in 1901 Gresley spent the summer season at Blackpool's locomotive running shed. He then moved on to Newton Heath where, in 1904, he became the Assistant Superintendent of the Carriage and Wagon Works.

In February 1905 he was appointed the Carriage and Wagon Superintendent at the GNR's Doncaster Works. His first design consisted of two steam-powered

◁ This beautifully executed line drawing of Patrick Stirling's 2-2-2 locomotive No.234 was completed by Nigel Gresley at the age of just 13. (Author's Collection)

▽ Sir Nigel Gresley, one of Great Britain's most famous steam locomotive engineers, is seen admiring his eponymous streamlined A4 class Pacific locomotive No.4498 at King's Cross depot, on the day of the formal naming of the locomotive during 1937. (David Ward Collection)

rail-motor cars which used valve gear driven by external Walschaerts motion, the first time that derived-motion was ever used by the GNR. It was much easier to adjust and maintain the mechanics of the vehicle rather than with the internal type that he'd been used to working with, and he subsequently used the design on most of his locomotives.

◀ Two locomotives built for the GNR, a 2-2-2 and a 4-2-2, are seen double-heading the forerunner of the 'Flying Scotsman' train on the East Coast route. Not only would *Flying Scotsman* ultimately replace these two locomotives, but it would complete the journey from King's Cross to Edinburgh non-stop and in a quicker time. (Author's Collection)

◀ Pennsylvania Railroad's K4s class Pacific steam passenger locomotive No.3750, is one of only two survivors of a fleet that once numbered 425 examples. It is seen awaiting attention at the Railroad Museum of Pennsylvania in Strasburg, during 2011. It was this type of locomotive that H.N. Gresley used as the basis of his design for his A1 class Pacific locomotives, of which *Flying Scotsman* was the third example to be completed. (Author)

In 1907 he produced some articulated coaches for suburban and main-line services which were very successful. This method of articulated bogies was subsequently incorporated into the design for Eurostar trains on Channel Tunnel rail services in Europe.

When H.A. Ivatt retired in 1911, Gresley was appointed Locomotive Engineer of the GNR. Main-line express passenger services were quickly reaching the hauling capacity limits of the large-boilered Atlantics, and so Gresley was under pressure to rectify this situation.

A3 class locomotive No.2750 *Papyrus* was built at Doncaster Works in 1929, and on 5 March 1935, together with a six-car train weighing 217 gross tons, passed Little Bytham, 4 miles south of Corby in Lincolnshire, at 106mph on its way down Stoke Bank, reaching a maximum speed of 108mph as it passed through Essendine. Towards the end of steam in the UK *Papyrus* was scrapped after being withdrawn from service on 9 September 1963. (David Ward Collection)

Did You Know?

The construction of *Flying Scotsman* was started by the Great Northern Railway in 1922.

Gresley's new Pacific 1470 class proved itself to be popular early on, when Engine Order No.297 was placed at Doncaster Works on 10 July 1922 for a further ten locomotives to be constructed. The first of this batch was destined to become *Flying Scotsman*.

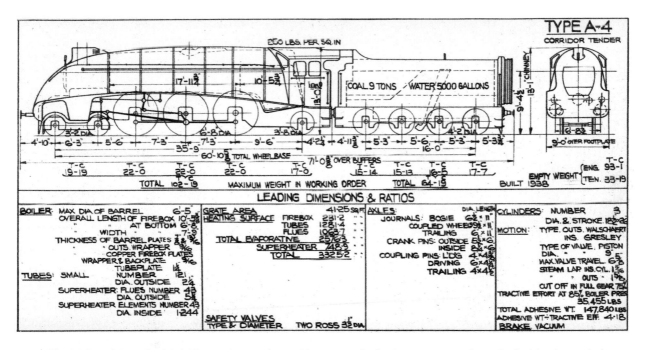

TYPE A-4

CORRIDOR TENDER

250 LBS. PER SQ. IN

COAL 9 TONS   WATER 5000 GALLONS

17'-11¾"   10'-5¼"

3'-2 DIA.   6-8 DIA.   6-8 DIA.   4'-2 DIA.   6'-8½"

9'-0 OVER FOOTPLATE

4'-10"   6'-3"   5'-6"   7'-3"   7'-3"   9'-6"   4'-2¼"   4'-11¾"   5'-3"   5'-6"   5'-3"   5'-3½"

35'-9   16'-0"

60'-10⅝" TOTAL WHEELBASE   7'-0⅝" OVER BUFFERS

| T-C 19-19 | T-C 22-0 | T-C 22-0 | T-C 22-0 | T-C 17-0 | T-C 15-14 | T-C 15-13 | T-C 16-5 | T-C 17-7 |

EMPTY WEIGHT { ENG. 93-1 / TEN. 33-19

TOTAL 102-19   MAXIMUM WEIGHT IN WORKING ORDER   TOTAL 64-19   BUILT 1938

LEADING DIMENSIONS & RATIOS

BOILER:
MAX DIA OF BARREL 6'-5"
OVERALL LENGTH OF FIREBOX 10'-5⅞"
" AT BOTTOM 6'-8"
" WIDTH " 7'-8"
THICKNESS OF BARREL PLATES ⅞ & ⁹⁄₁₆
" OUTS. WRAPPER ⁵⁄₁₆
" COPPER FIREBOX PLATES ⁵⁄₁₆
WRAPPER & BACKPLATE ⁵⁄₁₆
TUBEPLATE 1¼

TUBES: SMALL NUMBER 121
DIA. OUTSIDE 2¼
SUPERHEATER: FLUES NUMBER 43
DIA. OUTSIDE 5¼
SUPERHEATER ELEMENTS NUMBER 43
DIA. INSIDE 1.244

GRATE AREA 41.25 SQ.FT
HEATING SURFACE FIREBOX 231.2 " "
TUBES 1281.4 " "
FLUES 1063.7 " "
TOTAL EVAPORATIVE 2576.3 " "
SUPERHEATER 748.9 " "
TOTAL 3325.2 " "

SAFETY VALVES
TYPE & DIAMETER   TWO ROSS 3½ DIA

AXLES: DIA. LENGTH
JOURNALS: BOGIE 6½ × 11"
COUPLED WHEELS 9½ × 11"
TRAILING 6 × 11"
CRANK PINS: OUTSIDE 5¾ × 6"
INSIDE 8¼ × 6"
COUPLING PINS: L'DG 4 × 4½
DRIVING 6 × 4½
TRAILING 4 × 4½

CYLINDERS: NUMBER 3
DIA. & STROKE 18½ × 26
MOTION: TYPE. OUTS. WALSCHAERT
INS. GRESLEY
TYPE OF VALVE. PISTON
DIA. " 9"
MAX.VALVE TRAVEL 6⅝
STEAM LAP INS.CYL. 1⁹⁄₁₆
" OUTS 1¾
CUT OFF IN FULL GEAR 75⁄
TRACTIVE EFFORT AT 85% BOILER PRES
35,455 LBS
TOTAL ADHESIVE WT. 147,840 LBS
ADHESIVE WT÷TRACTIVE EFF. 4·18
BRAKE VACUUM

△ The A4 class of streamlined 4-6-2 locomotive was designed by H.N. Gresley for the LNER in 1935, being the final development of his Pacific series after the success of *Flying Scotsman* and other class members. The streamlined design, with internal improvements, gave them high-speed capability as well as making them instantly recognisable, and one of the class, No.4468 *Mallard*, still holds the official record as the fastest steam locomotive in the world. Thirty-five of the class were built to haul the streamlined trains and express passenger trains on the East Coast Main Line route from King's Cross via York and Newcastle to Edinburgh. This drawing shows the general arrangement of an A4 class locomotive; many similarities to *Flying Scotsman* may be observed. (Peter Townend Collection)

He decided that a 4-6-2 wheel arrangement was the best way ahead and his initial design project of 1915 was for an elongated version of the Atlantic design, but using four cylinders. However, he had reached a design impasse and took as his model the new American Pennsylvania Railroad's 2-cylinder Pacific K4s class of 1914 (the 's' indicated that the locomotive was 'superheated').

Did You Know?
Flying Scotsman cost £7,944 to construct and was the third locomotive of its class to be completed.
On 23 October 1922, the frames of Gresley's Pacific – which was given works number 1564 – were laid down in the erecting shop of the GNR's Doncaster Works. Upon completion it was given the running number 1472 and would soon be named *Flying Scotsman*.

This locomotive gave Gresley some of the elements needed to design a thoroughly 'up-to-date' locomotive.

H.N. Gresley's first Pacific, No.1470, entered service in April 1922, with the second, No.1471, arriving in July 1922. The design was deemed to be revolutionary and successful by the GNR Board of Directors, who placed an order for a batch of ten further locomotives of this design to be constructed.

Between 1923 and 1925 a further fifty-one A1 class locomotives – by then re-designated from the 1470 class – were completed. Under Gresley, there followed a complete redesign of the valve gear on the A1 class and this was applied to all members of the class. Modified locomotives were given the designation of A3 class, with twenty-seven of the A1 class locomotives being rebuilt as A3s between 1928 and 1935.

The acceleration of the non-stop 'Flying Scotsman' service in 1932 from

8¼ to 7½ hours was an indication of changing railway management policy, with a continuing emphasis on speed as an incentive to passenger travel, especially during a period of trade depression and increasing competition from road transport.

Gresley then built a series of brand new A3 class locomotives, one of which (No.2750 *Papyrus*) reached a maximum speed of 108mph.

To work the new express passenger train service between King's Cross and Newcastle – the 'Silver Jubilee', named in celebration of the twenty-fifth year of King George V's reign – the LNER authorised Gresley to produce a streamlined development of his A3 class. Initially four locomotives were built and were given the designation of A4 class. All had the word 'silver' as part of their names.

During a press run to promote the service, No.2509 *Silver Link* twice achieved a speed of 112.5mph, breaking the British speed record as well as sustaining an average speed of 100mph over a distance of 43 miles. Following the commercial success of the 'Silver Jubilee' train, other streamlined services were introduced for which more A4s were built. One of the class, No.4468 *Mallard*, achieved the official record of being 'the fastest steam locomotive in the world', having reached the amazing speed of 126mph – a record it still holds.

H.N. Gresley, who had become Sir Nigel Gresley in 1936, died in office on 5 April 1941 at his home at Watton-at-Stone at the age of 65 and is buried in Netherseal, Derbyshire. He designed some of the world's most successful and famous steam locomotives, considered by many to be elegant both aesthetically and mechanically. His amazing innovations enabled passenger rail travel to be improved in speed, comfort and safety.

By the 1840s it was possible to travel from Yorkshire to London by rail, but the journey was long and circuitous, via Derby and Rugby to Euston. The London and York Railway proposed that a route should be constructed from London heading directly north and passing through Peterborough, Grantham and Doncaster.

Plans for the London Terminus – subsequently to be known as King's Cross, were first made in December 1848 under the direction of George Turnbull, the resident engineer for the construction of the first 20 miles of the GNR out of London. The main part of the station, which today includes platforms 1 to 8, was opened on 14 October 1852 and replaced a temporary terminus at Maiden Lane that had opened on 7 August 1850.

The initial climb out of London was severe, with gradients of 1 in 105/110 for quite a few miles, after which there were very few gradients exceeding 1 in 200 for significant stretches elsewhere on the main line.

When train services started, the earliest locomotives ordered for the GNR were of standard types built by well-known makers of the time. The relative lateness of the GNR's entry into the market gave it an advantage in that standard designs had evolved and improved. These locomotives were small and had 5ft 6in driving wheels, with boilers working at 90lb psi. Archibald Sturrock, who was the Locomotive Superintendent of the GNR from 1850 until 1866, having been Daniel Gooch's assistant on the GWR from 1840, fitted compensating levers on these primitive engines and this assisted them in running on the relatively poor and light-weight track. The compensating levers equalised the weight between the coupled axles and the outside-framed bogie also had compensating levers which carried about a third of the locomotive's weight.

Technological progress moved the design of steam locomotives on, leading to a notable locomotive on express duties: that of Patrick Stirling's 4-2-2 Single, a locomotive with 8ft driving wheels. Stirling had moved to the GNR in 1866 and designed his original Single in 1870 for speed and power on the GNR main line from London to York.

Henry Ivatt had the daunting task of replacing the venerable Patrick Stirling as the head of the GNR's locomotive department. But by the turn of the century the 'single-wheelers' were being taxed by increasing train loadings. Seeking greater power and adhesion, Ivatt took the American route and in 1897, with inspiration borrowed from the Baldwin Locomotive Works design for the Atlantic Coast Line in North

America, designed the first 4-4-2 or Atlantic type of locomotive to enter service in Great Britain. In 1898, twenty-eight years after Patrick Stirling's first 4-2-2 had appeared from Doncaster Works, Britain's first 4-4-2 Atlantic locomotive – No.990 – was ready for work.

Did You Know?

Flying Scotsman was the first steam locomotive to be completed for the newly formed London and North Eastern Railway in 1923.

On 7 February 1923 and un-named at this stage, the first of the batch of a further ten Pacific locomotives which had been authorised the previous year was completed. It became the first express passenger locomotive for the newly formed LNER. Turned out in apple green livery, it was coupled to an eight-wheeled tender No.5223 of GNR design and had the letters L&NER painted on the tender tank sides, above the number 1472.

One of the first pictures taken of the first express passenger locomotive to be completed for the newly formed L&NER, namely No.1472. At this time it had not yet been named *Flying Scotsman*. (Sir William McAlpine Collection)

No.4472 *Flying Scotsman* is seen at Doncaster Works, after it had been wrapped up in a hessian cover to preserve its immaculate shine, just prior to its departure for Wembley, where it was exhibited at the British Empire Exhibition during 1924. (Sir William McAlpine Collection)

Did You Know?

Flying Scotsman was something of a flagship locomotive for the London and North Eastern Railway. In February 1924, No.1472 acquired the name of *Flying Scotsman* and received the new running number of No.4472. Prepared to exhibition standards, *Flying Scotsman* then represented the LNER Company at the British Empire Exhibition at Wembley in 1924 and 1925. From then on, it was frequently used for promotional purposes.

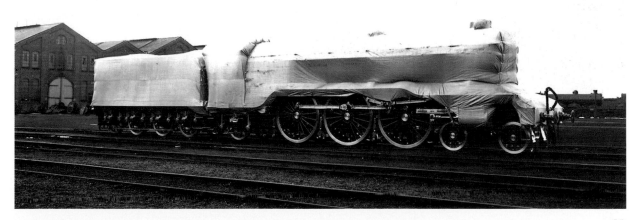

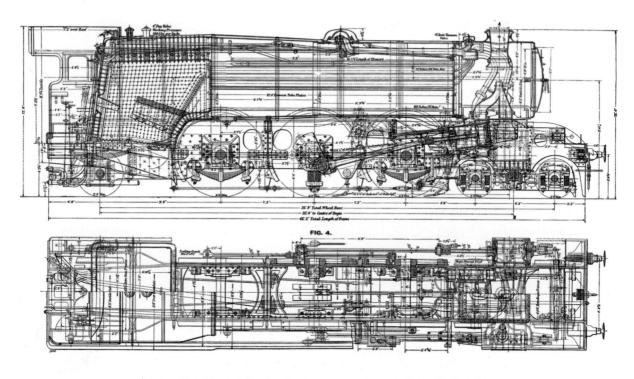

FIG. 4.

▲ A beautifully detailed drawing showing the general layout of H.N. Gresley's A1 class Pacific locomotive of the early 1920s. (Author's Collection)

The first production Atlantics proved to be fast and lively runners; so lively, in fact, that Ivatt had to caution his drivers to rein in the speed because stretches of the track between London and Doncaster were considered too uneven for safety's sake (with regards to high-speed running)!

The development of steam locomotives on the GNR continued with the introduction of large boilered Atlantics, which were the first engines to be built with a wide firebox and were a development from the first Atlantics.

No.251 became symbolic of the GNR and featured in most of the GNR's advertising and on timetable covers.

When H.N. Gresley was appointed the Locomotive Engineer of the GNR, he began thinking about large express passenger locomotives and became interested in 3-cylinder designs, which prompted him to design his famous conjugated valve gear. This operated the valve for the

Did You Know?

On 1 May 1928 at 10:00, the Lord Mayor of London waved the third of H.N. Gresley's A1 class locomotives, No.4472 *Flying Scotsman* and its train into history, as No.4472 worked the inaugural non-stop 'Flying Scotsman' service from King's Cross into Edinburgh Waverley, at 392.7 miles in 8 hours 3 minutes, with 386 tons tare.

middle cylinder from the motion of the two outside cylinders and was patented in November 1915. With the outbreak of the First World War the design for an express passenger locomotive had to be shelved, but Gresley tested the new conjugated valve gear with a 3-cylinder 2-8-0 locomotive, which was completed in 1918. This was followed by a much-needed 3-cylinder express goods 2-6-0 locomotive known as K3 class, which used a simpler version of the conjugated gear.

In 1920, Gresley was able to return to his plans for an express passenger Pacific locomotive, which by now included his conjugated valve gear. The K3 class exhibited valve 'over-run' at high speeds, so the maximum travel was reduced, which in turn reduced the locomotive's performance – but he was learning what could be achieved with his conjugated valve gear.

His Pacific boiler design was inspired by the Pennsylvania Railroad's K4s class Pacific locomotive. The boiler was reduced to the GNR's loading gauge but still kept a tapered shape and had tubes less than 19ft long.

Did You Know?

Flying Scotsman had a tender that included a corridor connection and tunnel through the water tank, giving access to the locomotive cab from the train, permitting the replacement of the driver and fireman without stopping the train.

For the introduction of the non-stop 'Flying Scotsman' service on 1 May 1928, ten special corridor tenders were built with a coal capacity of 9 tons instead of the usual 8 tons. Means to access the locomotive from the train through a narrow passageway inside the tender tank were provided, plus a flexible bellows connection linking it with the leading coach. The passageway, which ran along the right-hand side of the tender, was 5ft high and 18in wide.

On 10 January 1921, the GNR issued Engine Order No.293, giving Doncaster Works authority to construct two of Gresley's designed express Pacific tender locomotives.

On 30 March 1922, H.N. Gresley put the first of his 3-cylinder Pacific locomotives to work on the GNR. Apart from the solitary GWR locomotive No.111 *Great Bear*, it was the first 4-6-2 locomotive to be built in this country and was designed to work the fastest and heaviest trains on the GNR, although the North Eastern Railway soon had some examples of their own to compete with the Pacific.

Gresley's class became categorised as A1 class and were very different from the existing GNR locos, with large cabs and, for the first time in locomotive history, seats for the footplate crew. All this caused a sensation and provoked great interest amongst the public and railway worlds alike when they first arrived.

Gresley's Pacifics had three cylinders, which all drove the second coupled axle, which were driven by two outside sets of Walschaerts valve gear, with the middle valve being driven by Gresley conjugated valve gear, which was derived from the outside sets. With his new Pacific design H.N. Gresley had transformed locomotive traction on the East Coast Main Line.

The grouping of Britain's railways in 1923 into the 'Big Four' was intended to stem the losses being made by many of the country's 120 railway companies and resulted in four large companies, of which the LNER was the second largest with a total route mileage of 6,590 miles. No.1472, being one of the ten Pacific locomotives commissioned by the GNR, left Doncaster Works on 7 February 1923 with works number 1564, ready for service.

On 24 February 1923, No.1472 was allocated to its first depot of Doncaster and entered service, but on 27 December 1923 it returned to Doncaster Works for repair because of a fractured centre piston rod. As the replacement was going to take some time, it was chosen by the LNER to be its exhibit for the British Empire Exhibition at Wembley during 1924.

➤ When the LNER's A1 class locomotive No.4472 *Flying Scotsman* was exhibited at the British Empire Exhibition a souvenir book was produced about it. (Author's Collection)

THE
LONDON AND NORTH EASTERN
RAILWAY COMPANY

Three-Cylinder Superheated
4-6-2 PACIFIC TYPE
Express Tender Locomotive

Exhibited at the
BRITISH EMPIRE EXHIBITION
WEMBLEY
1924

No.1472 entered Doncaster Works for preparation to exhibition standards during which it was prepared in the new LNER's apple green livery. In addition, an LNER coat of arms was mounted on the cab sides of the locomotive; brass trim was added to the wheel splashers, and the tyres and motion had been highly burnished with the copper and brass fittings brightly polished. Its tender had the letters LNER surmounting the number 4472 on the sides.

Did You Know?

During the British Railways era, as well as working services into and out of King's Cross and Marylebone Stations, *Flying Scotsman* was also noted working services into St Pancras.

On 6 February 1924 it was renumbered and became No.4472. It was also fitted with nameplates bearing the words *Flying Scotsman* and was put on display to the public in the Palace of Engineering. Other railway exhibits included GWR-designed Castle class 4-6-0 No.4073 *Caerphilly Castle*, Stockton and Darlington Railway No.1 *Locomotion* and London's Metropolitan Railway, displaying one of their latest Inner Circle Underground cars – a first-class driving trailer built in 1923.

Opened on St George's Day (23 April) 1924, the British Empire Exhibition was the largest exhibition ever produced anywhere in the world at that time, costing £12 million to stage. It was opened by King George V, and every one of the fifty-eight countries that comprised the British Empire took part (with the exceptions of Gambia and Gibraltar). During the six months that it was open, an amazing 27 million visitors

45

During 1925, No.4472 *Flying Scotsman* was put on display for a second time at the British Empire Exhibition, Wembley. Also on display was GWR Castle class 4-6-0 locomotive No.4079 *Pendennis Castle*. The two locomotives are seen together once again when No.4472 *Flying Scotsman* had just moved to its new base at Market Overton, joining *Pendennis Castle*. At this time both locomotives were owned by W.H. McAlpine. (Sir William McAlpine Collection)

This colour postcard of No.4472 *Flying Scotsman* shows how it looked when it was exhibited at the British Empire Exhibition. (Author's Collection)

> On 5 April 1928, No.4472 *Flying Scotsman* left Doncaster Works after a general repair, during which it had been converted from the generous GNR loading gauge to the LNER loading gauge, enabling it greater route availability. This advert, dated May 1937, in *The Locomotive* magazine, shows where *Flying Scotsman*'s safety valves came from. (Author's Collection)

THE LOCOMOTIVE   iv   May 15, 1937

R.L.ROSS & C? L??
Premier Works Stockport

L N E R   4472

POP SAFETY VALVES
(Reduced Height Type)

Supplied by the Patentees and Manufacturers

toured the site – amazing for a country with a population of just 44,095,601!

After the exhibition ended, *Flying Scotsman* entered Doncaster Works for a 'heavy repair' and was prepared for its second tour of duty at the British Empire Exhibition at Wembley. On 9 May 1925, *Flying Scotsman* was put on display to the public for the second time.

On 17 April 1925, H.N. Gresley announced that the LNER and GWR would run comparative exchange trials between their two types of locomotives between Paddington and Plymouth. These, and other exchanges, were the direct outcome of the British Empire Exhibition at Wembley, where both railways had claimed that their locomotive was the more powerful.

So, during April and May 1925, GWR 4-6-0 No.4079 *Pendennis Castle* ran trials

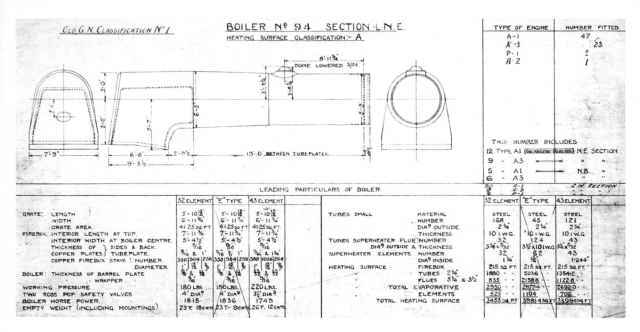

During the April 1928 general repair, boiler No.7693 was changed, as would be normal practice, and boiler No.7878 fitted. This had a 1in reduction in the height of the dome. The chimney, cab and safety valves were also either replaced or reduced in height. Short travel was replaced with long-travel valve gear and the variable blast-pipe was removed. The cab-side cutouts were changed to a higher level to accommodate bucket seats. This boiler drawing shows the difference in dome height. (Peter Townend Collection)

against H.N. Gresley's A1 class Pacific No.2545 *Diamond Jubilee*. The weeks of locomotive exchanges between the LNER and GWR in 1925 probably had a more profound influence on British locomotive engineering in general than any other comparable event in locomotive history.

In concluding the tests the GWR locomotives emerged more economical, with their superiority being attributed to a higher boiler pressure and, in particular, to better valve gear. The LNER learned valuable lessons from these trials, which resulted in a series of modifications being carried out from 1926 onwards on No.4477 *Gay Crusader*, which were eventually adapted for all of Gresley's Pacifics, improving their performance.

Did You Know?

As well as working normal passenger, parcels, high-speed fish and 'Flying Scotsman' services under British Railways, *Flying Scotsman* was also noted working the 'Aberdonian', 'Car Sleeper Ltd', 'Heart of Midlothian', 'Master Cutler', 'Norseman', 'Queen of Scots', 'South Yorkshireman', 'Talisman', 'Tees-Thames', 'Tees-Tyne Pullman', 'Scarborough Flyer', 'Tyne Commonwealth Quay', 'Tynesider', 'Yorkshire Pullman', 'West Riding Ltd' and 'White Rose' services.

▲ A view of No.4472 *Flying Scotsman* on 1 May 1928, just before it goes 'off-shed' to work the inaugural non-stop 'Flying Scotsman' service from King's Cross to Edinburgh Waverley. The 392.7 miles was covered in 8 hours 3 minutes, with 386 tons tare. (Author's Collection)

◀ *The Flying Scotsman* film was the first talkie film to be produced in England. Staring a young Raymond Milland in the role of the young fireman Jim, who falls in love with the old driver's daughter, the film is famous for some very daring stunt work done on the train itself. Here we see Ray Milland wearing a light coat and a trilby, looking at *Flying Scotsman* during the occasion of a trip celebrating the sixtieth anniversary of being built. (Sir William McAlpine Collection)

◀ In 1934, No.4472 *Flying Scotsman* achieved 'the first officially authenticated run of 100 mph for a steam locomotive', when it worked a test train running down Stoke Bank, south of Grantham. It is seen here at speed on that actual run on 30 November 1934. (Sir William McAlpine Collection)

No.4472 *Flying Scotsman* returned to normal main-line service in November 1925 and settled down to the regular work of a Doncaster-based Pacific locomotive, working services mainly between Doncaster and London.

When *Flying Scotsman* left Doncaster Works on 5 April 1928 after a general repair, it had been converted from the generous GNR loading gauge to the LNER loading gauge, giving it greater route availability. The process involved replacing its original boiler – No.7693 – for a new boiler, No.7878, with its chimney, cab, dome and safety valves either being replaced or reduced in height. Short-travel valve gear was replaced with long-travel valve gear. The coats of arms on the cab sides were removed and its cab-side numbers were restored. The locomotive was coupled to corridor tender No.5323 which had the branding LNER on the tender sides.

The economy of the new A1 class locomotives now allowed a dramatic change in train working procedures; in 1922, the GNR referred to the 10:00 departure from King's Cross as the 'East Coast Luncheon and Dining Car Express'. In the timetable of the LNER from 1923 until 10 July 1927, the 10:00 was called the 'Restaurant Car Express', and from 11 July 1927 the 10:00 departure to Scotland originally shown as the 'Restaurant Car Express' was officially renamed and became the 'Flying Scotsman'.

The running arrangements of the service were altered to make it become the longest 'non-stop' passenger service in railway history and in 1928 *Flying Scotsman* worked the inaugural non-stop service from London to Edinburgh in 8 hours 3 minutes, with 386 tons tare. Top-shed driver Albert Pibworth changed over with Gateshead driver Tom Blades through the newly designed corridor tender at Tollerton, just north of York. With

⏶ With such a lot of platform furniture in the foreground and a smoky industrial background, No.4472 *Flying Scotsman* is almost lost in this wintry scene taken at Newcastle in February 1936. (W.B. Greenfield, courtesy of the NELPG)

this name and using a corridor tender, it was able to run the 392 miles without stopping.

The development of troughs laid between the running lines enabled locomotives such as *Flying Scotsman* to complete non-stop runs from London to Edinburgh and so save valuable time for passengers.

In April 1929, No.4472 *Flying Scotsman* starred in the first sound feature film to be produced in this country – *The Flying Scotsman*, directed by Castleton Knight.

No.4472, *Flying Scotsman*, was used by the film company for six weeks of filming, with the film crews using numerous camera positions on the locomotive, tender and rolling stock.

No.4472 continued to work the non-stop 'Flying Scotsman' service into the 1930s as well as working normal passenger services and 'bread and butter' duties, including high-speed 'fish and meat' services that had originated from Aberdeen into King's Cross goods depot.

Then, on 30 November 1934, departing from King's Cross at 09.08, No.4472 *Flying Scotsman* made a high-speed test run to Leeds with '6-on' – that's six carriages – at 145 tons tare and covered a distance of 185.8 miles in 151 minutes 56 seconds. The return trip was achieved in 157 minutes 17 seconds with a load of 205.25 tons tare, officially achieving 100mph as it descended Stoke Bank near Grantham, becoming the first steam engine authenticated in the world to do so. Driver Sparshatt and Fireman Webster were used for both trips. By this time No.4472 had completed 653,000 miles since entering service and 44,176 miles since its last general repair.

Flying Scotsman was then back on prestigious train duties working the 'Harrogate Sunday Pullman'; 'Queen of Scots', 'West Riding' and 'Yorkshire Pullman' services until November 1939, when it entered Doncaster Works for a general repair.

No.4472 *Flying Scotsman* was briefly on 'station-pilot' duties in February 1940 and continued to work services into and out of King's Cross. On 3 April 1943, No.4472 left Doncaster Works after a general repair, during which it was repainted in wartime unlined black livery with the letters NE on the tender.

In 1945, Edward Thompson rebuilt the first A1 class locomotive No.4470 *Great*

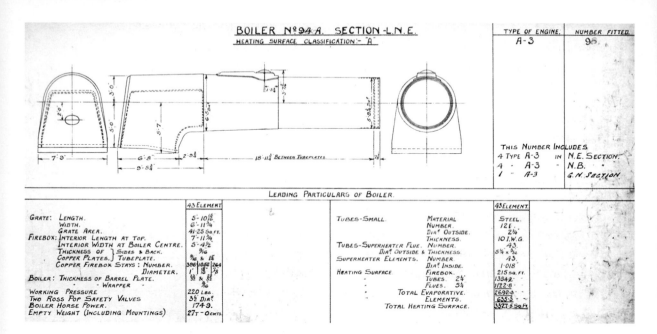

BOILER Nº 94 A. SECTION - L.N.E.

HEATING SURFACE CLASSIFICATION:- "A"

TYPE OF ENGINE.	NUMBER FITTED.
A-3	98.

THIS NUMBER INCLUDES
4 TYPE A-3 IN N.E. SECTION.
4 " A-3 " N.B. "
1 " A-3 " G.N. SECTION.

18-11¾ BETWEEN TUBEPLATES

LEADING PARTICULARS OF BOILER.

		43 ELEMENT				43 ELEMENT
GRATE:	LENGTH.	5'-10⅞	TUBES - SMALL.	MATERIAL		STEEL.
	WIDTH.	6'-11¾		NUMBER.		121.
	GRATE AREA.	41·25 Sq FT.		DIAᵗ OUTSIDE.		2¼
FIREBOX:	INTERIOR LENGTH AT TOP.	7'-11¾		THICKNESS.		10 I.W.G.
	INTERIOR WIDTH AT BOILER CENTRE.	5'-4½	TUBES - SUPERHEATER FLUE.	NUMBER.		43.
	THICKNESS OF } SIDES & BACK.	⁹⁄₁₆		DIAᵗ OUTSIDE & THICKNESS.		5⅛ x ³⁄₃₂
	COPPER PLATES.} TUBEPLATE.	⁹⁄₁₆ & 1⅛	SUPERHEATER ELEMENTS.	NUMBER.		43.
	COPPER FIREBOX STAYS : NUMBER.	386 1068 264		DIAᵗ INSIDE.		1·018
	DIAMETER.	1" 1⅛ ⅞	HEATING SURFACE	FIREBOX.		215 Sq. FT.
BOILER:	THICKNESS OF BARREL PLATE.	⅝ & ⅝		TUBES. 2¼		1334·2
	" WRAPPER "	³⁄₁₆		FLUES. 5⅛		1122·8
WORKING PRESSURE		220 Lbs.		TOTAL EVAPORATIVE.		2692·0
TWO ROSS POP SAFETY VALVES		3½ DIAᵗ		ELEMENTS.		635·3
BOILER HORSE POWER.		1749.		TOTAL HEATING SURFACE.		3327·3 Sq FT.
EMPTY WEIGHT (INCLUDING MOUNTINGS)		27ᴛ - 0ᴄᴡᴛꜱ.				

On 18 November 1946, by now an A10 class Pacific, No.103 *Flying Scotsman* entered Doncaster Works for a general repair and rebuilding, to become an A3 class locomotive and returned to traffic on 4 January 1947. It had exchanged its boiler, No.7785 – previously fitted to class mate No.2561 *Minoru* – for boiler No.8078, which was previously fitted to No.2576 *The White Knight*. This became the sixth boiler it had carried. This drawing shows the details of the boiler of *Flying Scotsman* as an A3 class locomotive with banjo dome. (Peter Townend Collection)

Northern, which was initially kept classified as an A1 class locomotive, and on 25 April 1945, the seventeen surviving A1 class 4-6-2s, including No.4472 *Flying Scotsman*, were reclassified to become A10 class. The intention was always to rebuild the remaining A10s into the new A1 class; however, this was not done as the rebuild was not successful. Instead they were rebuilt to become A3 class locomotives, with the A10 class becoming extinct in 1948.

No.4472's duties then became quite varied and on 24 April 1946, *Flying Scotsman* was renumbered to become No.502. But less than two weeks later, on 5 May 1946, it was renumbered again and became No.103. In the middle of all this, on 5 April 1941, Sir Nigel Gresley died of a heart attack, just two months before he was due to retire.

On 4 January 1947, No.103 *Flying Scotsman* returned to traffic, having been rebuilt at Doncaster Works from an A10 class into an A3 class locomotive. In this reclassification it exchanged its boiler, No.7785, for boiler No.8078, which became the sixth boiler that it had carried since new. This new boiler had a pressure of 220lb psi compared with 180lb psi in the A1 and A10 class boilers, and it was fitted with a 'banjo dome' – which is basically an elongated form of steam collector developed to help prevent priming water carry-over to the pistons. It was developed by H.N. Gresley from Patrick Stirling's '8-footers'. The tractive effort had been increased from 26,926lb to 32,910lb and No.103 was repainted with LNER apple green livery, lined out in black and white.

The magic date for the start of the rebuilding of Britain's railway network after the Second World War was 1 January 1948. British Railways came into being (later trading as British Rail) and was the operator of British railway systems originating from the nationalisation of the 'Big Four' railway companies until privatisation, which took place in stages between 1994 and 1997.

This period of nationalisation saw sweeping changes in the railway network, with steam traction being eliminated in favour of diesel and electric traction, passenger services replacing freight as the main source of business, and one-third of the network being axed.

Upon nationalisation, the former LNER was divided into three areas, becoming the new British Railways Eastern Region, North Eastern Region and part of the Scottish Region.

Did You Know?

When in revenue-earning service, *Flying Scotsman* would work non-stop trains from London to Edinburgh in 8¼ hours. Its tender held 5,000 gallons of water – enough for approximately 100 miles between fill ups – and carried 9 tons of coal. As it travelled, water was replenished by scooping it up from troughs laid between the rails. As steam engines disappeared from BR in the 1960s, so too did the water columns and the track water troughs. In 1966, Alan Pegler bought a second tender and had it converted to carry water only, increasing *Flying Scotsman*'s capacity to 6,000 gallons and giving a new range in total of over 200 miles.

On 15 March 1948, No.103 *Flying Scotsman*, now a nationalised asset, left Doncaster Works after a general repair, during which it had exchanged its boiler, the replacement being the seventh boiler that it had carried. The new boiler had a 'banjo dome' type of steam collector fitted and the maximum forward cut-off was increased from 65 to 75 per cent (in a steam engine, 'cut-off' is the point in the piston stroke at which the inlet valve is closed). No.103 had been painted in apple green livery and was renumbered to become No.E103, with the legend BRITISH RAILWAYS painted on the tender.

No.E103 was noted at Newcastle on 5 April 1948 and continued to work regular 'up and down' services to and from King's Cross, including 'The Yorkshire Pullman'. Then on 30 December 1948, No.E103 *Flying Scotsman* left Doncaster Works after receiving a light repair, where it had been renumbered once again to become No.60103, retaining its apple green livery.

legend on the tender. In this form, as well as performing its normal duties, No.60103 *Flying Scotsman* worked a 'Widnes *v.* Warrington' Rugby Cup Final special into King's Cross on 6 May 1950 (Warrington won 15–0).

By now *Flying Scotsman*'s shed code allocation had been changed to Leicester Central – 38C – and it could be seen working the 'Master Cutler' from Marylebone to Sheffield Victoria as well as various other services to Manchester and Nottingham.

Time again for another service in the works, but this time when No.60103 *Flying Scotsman* left Doncaster Works after a general repair and boiler swap it was painted in British Railways' dark green livery – actually called 'middle chrome green', not dissimilar in colour to the GWR's 'Brunswick Green' – and was outlined in black and orange. In this condition it regularly worked 'The South Yorkshireman' service into Marylebone.

On 16 December 1949, No.60103 *Flying Scotsman* left Doncaster Works after a general repair, during which it exchanged its boiler again and was painted in British Railways' blue livery, outlined in white and black. The early 'cycling lion' crest that was used on locomotives between 1949 and early 1956 replaced the BRITISH RAILWAYS

Flying Scotsman was one of the last right-hand drive A3 class locomotives still in active service and it was noted in this form on 28 February 1953 departing at 14:10 from Platform A at London Road Station in Manchester, which, after being extensively rebuilt, would be renamed Piccadilly Station in 1960. No.60103 travelled along the up eastern line towards Ardwick, with an express service into Marylebone. Its H.N. Gresley designed tender bore the original BR emblem on its sides.

In 1953, *Flying Scotsman's* depot was changed to Grantham and in April 1954, *Flying Scotsman* was finally converted to left-hand drive at Doncaster Works.

Notable services worked by *Flying Scotsman* in the 1950s were: 'Heart of Midlothian', 'Norseman', 'Northumbrian', 'Queen of Scots', 'Scarborough Flyer', 'Talisman', 'Tees-Tyne Pullman', 'Tyne Commission Quay', 'Tynesider', 'White Rose', 'Yorkshire Pullman' and of course the 'Flying Scotsman' – indeed, you name it and *Flying Scotsman* probably worked it.

When in Britain, travel as the British do!

YOU'LL find it part of the fun of your visit... learning to call the railroads "railways," the cars "carriages." And you'll enjoy riding in comfortable "compartments."

But even more, you'll be delighted with the *low cost* of traveling, sleeping, dining on British Railways. Imagine a full-course dinner . . . one that leaves you feeling blissful . . . for only $1.50!

The length and breadth of the United Kingdom, it is the *trains* that take you everywhere . . . and take you there, often, at 60 to 80 miles an hour. With very little strain on your budget!

The British take pride . . . with reason . . . in their *railways* as the way to get about the country, quickly and conveniently. Even long trips cost very little.

Especially for Americans, train travel in Britain and Ireland is a bargain. Before you leave home (they are *not* sold overseas) you can buy Thrift Coupons. Up to 1000 miles of travel for only $31.50 (1st class) $21 (2nd Class). Rates vary in Canada. Also good for Irish cross-channel, and Clyde and MacBrayne's steamers.

Your dollars will travel far-ther . . . and faster . . . on *British Railways!*

Thrift Coupons

Any Travel Agent can get you British Railway Thrift Coupons.

Want "planning" literature? Write British Railways, Dept. AO, 1 630 Fifth Avenue, New York 20, N. Y.

BRITISH RAILWAYS
OFFICES IN NEW YORK · CHICAGO · LOS ANGELES · TORONTO

◁ Here is an advert promoting British Railways' 'Thrift Coupons'. It was published in a North American newspaper during the 1960s. It used stereotypical clichés: a bowler-hatted city gent checking his watch – the train arriving on time – with a knowing look; and chatty, happy women. What a wonderful way to travel. The advert is completed by proudly showing the world famous name of the crack express: the 'Flying Scotsman'. (Author's Collection)

Did You Know?

Flying Scotsman featured in The Railway Series of children's books by the Revd W. Awdry, famous for Thomas the Tank Engine. In the book *Enterprising Engines*, *Flying Scotsman* visits the fictional Island of Sodor between 1967 and 1968 to cheer up his only surviving brother, Gordon. At this time *Flying Scotsman* had two tenders, and this was a key feature of the plot of one of the stories, called 'Tenders for Henry', where Henry was jealous.

So after all of this hard work, *Flying Scotsman* arrived back at Doncaster Works again on 10 December 1959 for another boiler change. But this time, when it left several weeks later, it was also the proud owner of a Kylchap double blast-pipe and a double chimney, all fitted at a cost of £153. The Kylchap system was designed and patented by French steam engineer André Chapelon, using a second-stage nozzle designed by the Finnish engineer Kyösti Kylälä and known as the Kylälä spreader; thus the name 'Kylchap' for this design. It was André Chapelon's theory that such a multi-stage mixing and suction arrangement would be more efficient than a single-stage arrangement then popular in steam locomotive draughting, as, instead of concentrating the suction on one specific location, it would guarantee a more even flow through the firetubes. However, although performance was improved, the fitting of this system caused a softer exhaust beat which in turn caused exhaust smoke to obscure the driver's vision.

Flying Scotsman continued to earn its keep and entered Doncaster Works once more for another boiler change; this time it emerged with the fourteenth boiler that it had carried.

On 10 April 1961, No.60103 *Flying Scotsman* worked the 14:00 King's Cross 'Tees-Thames' service, but its next showcase was on 6 May, when it worked the Gainsborough Model Railway Society's (GMRS) first-ever special, 'The Lake District Rail Tour'. Starting at Lincoln, the train travelled via Doncaster, York, Gateshead, Newcastle and Hexham to Carlisle and return. The GMRS would subsequently prove to get even more involved in the subsequent chapters detailing the history of *Flying Scotsman*.

Since the fitting of the double Kylchap blast-pipe and double chimney, smoke drifting over the cab of A3 class locomotives was becoming a major problem. Peter N.

Did You Know?

Flying Scotsman visited North America between 1969 and 1972.

When Alan Pegler bought *Flying Scotsman* in 1963 he was granted permission to run it on British Railways tracks for special excursions until 1972. But in 1969, before the contract ended, *Flying Scotsman*, its two tenders and an exhibition train of nine coaches left the UK to tour the US. Travelling some 15,400 miles, it also visited some towns and cities in neighbouring Canada.

Townend, the pragmatic Shedmaster of King's Cross, recommended to the 'powers that be' that German-style trough smoke

deflectors should be fitted to ease the problem. Several locomotives were so fitted and the experiment was deemed to be a total success.

On 16 December 1961, No.60103 *Flying Scotsman* left Doncaster Works after a casual light repair, during which it had been fitted with German-style trough *Witte*

▶ No.60103 *Flying Scotsman* at King's Cross Station during 1962, fitted with *Witte* trough smoke deflectors. They'd been fitted due to smoke obscuring the driver's vision after a double chimney had been fitted, and were deemed to be a complete success at deflecting smoke away from the cab. (Geoff Rixon)

▶▶ On 14 January 1963, No.60103 *Flying Scotsman*, with 11-on, worked its last official service under BR ownership: the 13:15 from King's Cross to Leeds service. No.60103 is seen prior to departure at King's Cross on this historic run. (D. Trevor Rowe)

smoke deflectors. Essentially they were a variation of one of two designs of the *Windleitbleche* smoke deflector originating from the Deutsche Reichsbahn-Gesellschaft – the German national railway – between the two world wars. No.60103 was then

cleaned and received a coat of BR dark green paint and returned to its home depot of King's Cross – shed code 34A.

Although *Flying Scotsman* continued its daily duties of working many passenger trains including: the 'Heart of Midlothian', 'Northumbrian', 'Queen of Scots', 'White Rose' and others, the service life of *Flying Scotsman* working for British Railways was coming to an end, with the wholesale introduction of diesel-electric-powered locomotives.

When *Flying Scotsman*'s last day of service finally arrived, something very special happened to this famous locomotive. Instead of going to the breaker's yard to be dismantled for scrap, it was sold to a private buyer who ran it on British Railways' tracks and in the process saved this icon for future generations to enjoy.

Did You Know?

Flying Scotsman travelled through the Panama Canal in 1973.

The North American tour started well, but by 1972 financial problems led to bankruptcy, with *Flying Scotsman* and its train being seized by the American Internal Revenue Service (IRS). No.4472 and its train were moved to Sharpe Army Base, Lathrop, California, for secure storage. Amid fears for *Flying Scotsman*'s future, William McAlpine stepped in and bought the locomotive, returning it to Liverpool, England, via the Panama Canal in February 1973. It then moved to Derby Works under its own steam, where William McAlpine paid for the locomotive's restoration to running order.

Penny Pegler, daughter of Alan Pegler, explains how *Flying Scotsman* came into her life to change it forever: '… it was a snowy January evening in 1963 and I was 9 years old. My father came upstairs as always, to read me my bedside story, but when he popped his head around the door there was a twinkle in his eye. He often had a twinkle, but this seemed to be a special twinkle and was accompanied by a mischievous grin. He sat down on my bed, and whispered, "today I bought a steam engine! She is called *Flying Scotsman* and I will have her painted apple green".

He went on to describe how she was destined to be destroyed and that there were no identical engines anywhere in the world. He was stepping in to save her.

This all seemed perfectly natural to me, as Papa was amongst the saviours of my friend "Prince" and the Ffestiniog Railway, so I snuggled down to sleep imagining what adventures lay ahead of us, but wondering slightly where we would keep our bright green steam locomotive.

The problem was soon resolved: we were to use a shed in Doncaster. Saturday mornings would see us gathering up picnic baskets and cotton rags and driving off to "our shed", where we would clean and polish. At the end of the day we would say goodbye to 4472, as she had become, pile into the car and drive home with grimy clothes and happy faces.

By now she had been nicknamed "Scotty" and was part of the family. Little did we realise that this wonderful locomotive would change the course of our lives.'

Beginning in January 1961, Alan Pegler spent eighteen months in negotiations with BR to buy *Flying Scotsman*, subject to a condition that he was given permission 'to

In this compilation, we see some of the photographs that Alan Pegler took when he was a young schoolboy. The first picture was taken when Alan was aged just 8 years old in 1928 and the remainder were taken when he was 12.

1. Although slightly out of focus, Alan Pegler was just 8 years old when he took this photo on 1 May 1928, showing the very first Edinburgh to London 'Flying Scotsman' service worked by A1 class locomotive No.2580 *Shotover*.

2. Here a relief mail train is seen during Easter week in 1932, being worked by A1 class No.4472 *Flying Scotsman* shortly before it entered Doncaster Works for a general repair.

3. An up 'Flying Scotsman' service passes through Barnby Moor worked by an A1 class locomotive during 1932.

5. A fine view of A1 class locomotive No.4478 *Hermit* at Sutton-on-Trent, on the East Coast Main Line.

6. Here a London–Leeds express is seen at Babworth, worked by A1 class locomotive No.4473 *Solario* again during 1932.

7. A1 class locomotive No.4472 *Flying Scotsman* is seen at Babworth near Retford, working an Edinburgh–London express. Little did Alan Pegler know that thirty-one years later he would be the owner of this fine locomotive and that he would be running it over these same tracks working special charters for railway enthusiasts. (All images Penny Pegler Collection)

4. Another view at Barnby Moor as a slow Doncaster–London passenger service is seen worked by an Ivatt Atlantic No.4456, which had originally been completed at Doncaster Works in October 1910. No.4472 *Flying Scotsman* and its classmates were built to replace this type of locomotive due to the demands of increased loadings and speeds. Note the somersault signal over the dome of the locomotive.

> Here are the 'Heads of Agreement' between the British Railways Board and Alan Pegler, relating to the sale of *Flying Scotsman*. (David Ward Collection)

run it continuously from 1963 to 1972 as a private engine hauling passenger trains'.

On 14 January 1963, Alan Pegler travelled to King's Cross from Retford on the 'Master Cutler' Pullman service, arriving in London soon after 10:00 Transport had been laid on to take him out to 'Top Shed', where the preparation of No.60103 *Flying Scotsman*, in the middle of a big freeze, was captured by TV newsreel and press cameras. Alan's wife Pauline told the *Daily Sketch* newspaper: 'Trains are not just a hobby for my husband; you could call them a professional life interest.'

Having moved to the head of its train, No.60103 *Flying Scotsman* with 11-on then worked its last official passenger train service under BR ownership – the 13:15 from King's Cross to Leeds as far as Doncaster, where it came to a stand exactly six minutes early. No.60103 was taken off the service and moved to Doncaster Works, ending

'40-years minus 3 weeks' of public service since originally being completed in 1923. Upon entering the works, *Flying Scotsman* was introduced to the world of preservation.

During *Flying Scotsman*'s time inside Doncaster Works, it was restored as closely as possible to its former LNER condition: the German-style smoke deflectors were removed; the double chimney was replaced by a single chimney; the tender was replaced with one of the corridor type, similar to that with which it had run between 1928 and 1936 for the non-stop runs between King's Cross and Edinburgh Waverley, and it was repainted in its former LNER livery of apple green and had its former number No.4472 reinstated.

Part of the contract to buy *Flying Scotsman* allowed Alan Pegler to run it on BR tracks, with BR maintaining the locomotive in working order. With this in place, No.4472 *Flying Scotsman* was able

HEADS OF AGREEMENT

between the British Railways Board and Alan Francis Pegler, Esq.,
relating to the sale to him of the 'Flying Scotsman' railway locomotive.

1. In these Heads of Agreement:
   'the Board' means the British Railways Board and (where the context so admits) its legal successors;
   'the Purchaser' means Mr. Alan Francis Pegler and (where the context so admits) his successors in title;
   'the locomotive' means the Board's railway locomotive No. 60103 known as 'Flying Scotsman' and includes the tender thereof.

2. The Board will sell and the Purchaser will purchase free from incumbrances the locomotive at the price of Three thousand pounds (£3,000.0.0). The property in the locomotive will pass on delivery which will take place at noon on 16th April, 1963 at King's Cross Motive Power Depot, London.

3. Prior to delivery or as soon thereafter as may be the Board will at their own cost:
   (a) remove the existing smoke deflector plates from the locomotive;
   (b) replace the existing chimney and blast pipe by a single chimney and blast pipe similar to those with which the locomotive was formerly fitted;
   (c) replace the existing tender by a former L.N.E.R. corridor tender;
   (d) repaint the locomotive and the tender in L.N.E.R. express passenger locomotive colours;
   (e) restore to the locomotive its former number, viz: 4472;
   (f) ensure that the locomotive is in running order and carry out two satisfactory trial runs.

4. The locomotive when not in use upon the railway will be stabled in the Old Engine Weighhouse at Doncaster Loco. Works at an annual rent of Sixty five pounds (£65.0.0) or at such other place as the Board may from time to time determine. The Purchaser shall be liable for any rates from time to time payable in respect of such premises and in addition will bear the cost of keeping the same in good and substantial repair and condition to the satisfaction of the Board.

5. If the Purchaser, or any duly authorised representative of his, wishes to visit the locomotive while stabled or to carry out any inspection thereof he shall make the necessary arrangements with the Board's Works Manager, Doncaster. Apart from personnel of the Board who may in connection with the provisions hereof require so to do neither the Board nor the Purchaser shall without the consent of the other permit any other persons (and in particular any member of the public) to visit the locomotive while stabled.

6. The Purchaser shall from time to time and at his own cost make all necessary arrangements with the Board's Traffic Manager, Doncaster for the proper maintenance of the locomotive and all necessary periodical inspections thereof so as to ensure that the locomotive is kept in good repair and condition and that all legal requirements are complied with. However, as a matter of practical convenience whenever the locomotive is used for the purposes of the business of the Board in accordance with the provisions for hiring the locomotive contained in Clause 8 the Board will at a reasonable cost to the Purchaser properly maintain and repair the locomotive.

7. The locomotive will be stabled at the Purchaser's risk in all respects and it will be for the Purchaser, if he so desires, to effect any insurance with regard to the locomotive. In the event of a hiring out of the locomotive for the purposes of the business of the Board the Board shall keep the Purchaser fully indemnified against all actions claims and demands taken or made by any person and against any loss incurred by the Purchaser arising out of or in connection with any accident or event whatsoever occurring during the period of hiring so however that this indemnity shall not be construed as extending to the making good of any fair wear and tear.

8. Subject to Clause 13(a) in the event of:
   (a) the Purchaser wishing the locomotive to be run over any part of the Board's railway system; or
   (b) the Board wishing to use the locomotive;
   the Purchaser or the Board (as the case may be) shall give reasonable notice to the other of their proposal, together with all relevant information. If any such proposal is agreed between the parties the transaction (in so far as it relates to the user of the locomotive) shall take the form of a hiring of the locomotive to the Board from the Purchaser upon the terms and conditions then agreed between them. Each party shall have complete discretion either to refuse any proposal put forward by the other or only to agree thereto subject to such conditions as the Purchaser or the Board (as the case may be) think fit.

9. Subject to the provisions of Clauses 6, 8 and 13(a) hereof and to the provisions of this clause and except in the case of emergency no person may maintain, repair, drive or fire the locomotive, or ride thereon without the consent of the Board and the Purchaser. In particular the Board will not issue any footplate pass without first consulting the Purchaser. However nothing in these Heads of Agreement shall prevent the Board from authorising any of their personnel, in the course of their normal duties, to ride upon the footplate of the locomotive in connection with the proper discharge by the Board of any obligations arising under or by virtue of this Agreement.

10. The Board shall not at any time hereafter use or permit the use of the name 'Flying Scotsman' on or in connection with any steam locomotive owned or controlled by it in the United Kingdom but nothing herein contained shall prevent the Board from using such name to describe any train service run by it.

11. The Board hereby granted to the Purchaser full but non-exclusive royalty free licence to use the locomotive under any patents and registered designs covering the locomotive or any part thereof.

12. This Agreement other than Clauses 2 and 3 thereof may without prejudice to the accrued rights of either party be determined:
    (a) by either party giving to the other not less than twelve months' notice in writing expiring in or at any time after the Sixteenth day of April One thousand nine hundred and sixty six; or
    (b) forthwith by the Board in the event of any sum due hereunder by the Purchaser to the Board remaining unpaid for more than six months.

13. In the event of this Agreement being determined:
    (a) under Clause 12(a) hereof and by the time the notice has expired no arrangements have been made for the stabling of the locomotive elsewhere (for which purposes the Board shall provide all reasonable assistance and shall grant to the Purchaser the right to run the locomotive over the Board's railway system to such extent as may be necessary); or
    (b) under Clause 12(b) hereof;
    the Board may forthwith re-possess the locomotive and sell the same provided that the Board shall account to the Purchaser for any proceeds of sale less any sums properly due from the Purchaser to the Board, including the cost of such re-possession and sale.

DATED this Sixteenth day of April One thousand nine hundred and sixty three.

Signed
by the Purchaser ....

A classic view of a classic locomotive. No.4472 *Flying Scotsman* is seen on the Forth Railway Bridge during one of its many visits there during its ownership by Alan Pegler. (Author's Collection)

to work a considerable number of private charter rail tours all around the country.

During this period, the watering facilities for steam locomotives were fast disappearing, so Alan Pegler purchased a second corridor tender in September 1966. Retaining its side corridor, it was adapted as an auxiliary water tender with a capacity

Did You Know?
Flying Scotsman visited Australia between 1988 and 1989.
In October 1988, *Flying Scotsman* arrived in Australia to take part in that country's bicentenary celebrations as a central attraction in the Aus Steam '88 festival, where it travelled more than 28,000 miles over Australian rails.

of 6,000 gallons and cost Alan £6,000 to buy and convert, whereas the cost to buy *Flying Scotsman* alone had cost him £3,500.

In this form *Flying Scotsman* worked hundreds of rail tours all across the country during the ensuing years and in 1968, the year that steam traction officially ended on British Railways, *Flying Scotsman* ran non-stop from King's Cross to Edinburgh Waverley to commemorate the fortieth anniversary of the first non-stop 'Flying Scotsman' service.

By now *Flying Scotsman* was the only steam locomotive permitted to run on BR tracks and there was a lot of bad feeling with other steam locomotive owners, who did not have the same privilege.

So, before Alan Pegler's contract with BR ended, he hit upon the idea of taking *Flying Scotsman* to the USA and Canada to work an exhibition train.

➤ No.4472 *Flying Scotsman* worked a GMRS special on 12 September 1965 between Waterloo and Weymouth. It is seen here being turned on the Weymouth turntable in preparation for the return working via Yeovil into Paddington. (GMRS Collection, courtesy Joy and Richard Woods)

No.4472 *Flying Scotsman* worked 'The Retford Rover' on 21 May 1967 from King's Cross to Retford, where buses took passengers to Gainsborough to see the GMRS's famed model railway layout. The trip was organised by the GMRS along with Alan Pegler, seen here at King's Cross prior to departure. (Author's Collection)

This fine view of both of *Flying Scotsman*'s tenders was taken at Norwich during one of No.4472's visits there during the Alan Pegler era in the 1960s. (David Chappell)

Did You Know?

Flying Scotsman became the first steam locomotive to travel on the standard gauge Central Australia Railway.
Its Australian tour concluded with a return trans-continental run from Sydney to Perth via Alice Springs, in which it was the first steam engine to travel on the recently built standard gauge Central Australia Railway.

No.4472 *Flying Scotsman* is seen in undercoat grey at Doncaster Works having its bell filled in preparation for its North American tour. (Author's Collection)

No.4472 *Flying Scotsman* is ready for another turn of duty as it rests in its shed at Doncaster. It is fitted with a bell and large whistle, which had been installed in preparation for its imminent North American tour. (Frank Hornby)

During the winter of 1968–69, No.4472 *Flying Scotsman* visited the Hunslet Engine Company's Works in Leeds for a strip down and a heavy overhaul. This allowed the railway authorities from the USA and Canada to inspect it to their satisfaction before it was permitted to run in North America. It was then sent to Doncaster Works, where it was 'trial-fitted' with a 'pilot' (otherwise known as a cowcatcher), an American-style buckeye coupling and a high-intensity headlamp – which were later fitted on board the *Saxonia* on its journey to Boston – but a bell, an American-style whistle and air brakes were fitted before it was painted in apple green livery.

In 1969, No.4472 *Flying Scotsman*, its two tenders, a support coach, a reception car, four exhibition cars, two Pullman cars and an observation car left the UK on three transatlantic cargo ships. The tour started well and travelled to Boston, New

➤ *Flying Scotsman*'s first 'Trade Mission in North America' started in Boston on 8 October 1969. To assist this tour, two double-decker buses were converted into mobile sales kiosks and followed the route of the train, selling souvenirs at each stop. The image shows the ten specially selected girls that accompanied the buses acting as sales assistants with one of the buses in Battersea Park, London, on 9 September 1969. (Author's Collection)

York, Houston and even visited Canada. But the money for *Flying Scotsman* began to run out and so in a last-ditch attempt, San Francisco was visited until the spring of 1972. Around this time offers to exhibit *Flying Scotsman* in Japan, Australia and other countries were received, but Alan Pegler was finally declared bankrupt in 1972, with all of his assets, including *Flying Scotsman*, seized by the tax authorities.

Alan Pegler celebrated his 90th birthday on 16 April 2010 at the Ffestiniog Railway, North Wales with his friends and family

At Liverpool Docks, No.4472 *Flying Scotsman* was lifted from the shores of England and was loaded on the starboard side of the cargo ship *Saxonia* for its transatlantic journey to Boston. Many feared that *Flying Scotsman*'s trip would mean that it would never return home again. (Sir William McAlpine Collection)

The classic American cowcatcher is known in North America as a 'pilot'. Here is the pilot that went with *Flying Scotsman* on its North American tour. Constructed at Doncaster Works, it was fitted to *Flying Scotsman* on board *Saxonia* prior to its journey across the Atlantic Ocean. The pilot – which is now in the author's collection – is seen at Carnforth during 1999. (Author)

around him. I was fortunate enough to be included in this gathering, in celebration of a man who had the vision to save *Flying Scotsman*.

Alan died at his home in Stepney, East London on 18 March 2012 aged 91. He was the man who spent his own fortune to rescue *Flying Scotsman* from destruction – for future generations to admire and enjoy.

◄◄ With a very American background scene, No.4472 *Flying Scotsman* is in full flight as it works its exhibition train during the early stages of the North American tour. (Paul Dowie Collection)

◄ On 4 November 1969, No.4472 *Flying Scotsman* made a stop in the heart of Denison, Texas, and posed alongside Dwight D. Eisenhower's birthplace. Alan Pegler is seen leaning on one of *Flying Scotsman*'s buffers. (Paul Dowie Collection)

◄◄ Penny Pegler, daughter of Alan Pegler, is seen aged 17 with her father on the footplate of *Flying Scotsman*, during a stop at Montreal, Canada, on its North American tour, part two. (Penny Pegler Collection)

◄ A close-up view showing the detail of the bell and whistle that were fitted to *Flying Scotsman* during its North American tour. The bell – now part of the author's collection – has the inscription: 'Donated by the Southern Railway System 1969.' (Author's Collection)

▲ Over the weekend that it arrived in San Francisco, in March 1972, *Flying Scotsman* is seen at the San Francisco Maritime Park entrance situated at the Hyde & Beach Street's terminus of the Powell Street cable car line. San Francisco Bay is visible in the background. (Jack Neville)

◀◀ During 1971 and 1972, No.4472 *Flying Scotsman*, administration car, No.21177, Pullman Car, *Lydia* and observation car No.SC 281 worked trains at 10mph along the Embarcadero – the 'bell railroad' – at weekends from 10:00 until 18:00. The California Shell Fish Company looks exactly the same today. (Jack Neville)

◀ An interior view of the inside of the Victoria Station Restaurant at Universal Studios, California, not long after its original opening in 1977. The former *Flying Scotsman* exhibition train coaches are painted in unlined green and cream livery. (Paul Dowie Collection)

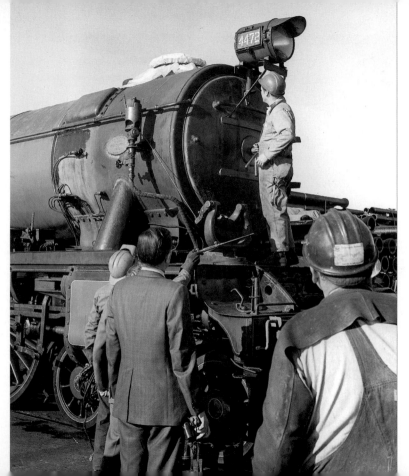

◁ January 1973 and No.4472 *Flying Scotsman* is seen on the dockside at Oakland, California, being prepared for shipment to Liverpool after being bought by Bill (later Sir William) McAlpine. (Paul Dowie Collection)

In the early 1970s fears arose for *Flying Scotsman*'s future in North America after the bankruptcy of Alan Pegler, with speculation that No.4472 could take up permanent residence there or even be cut up. Alan Bloom of Norfolk garden centre fame telephoned Bill McAlpine to discuss the matter.

George Hinchcliffe, who had run *Flying Scotsman* for Alan Pegler in North America, was asked by Bill to fly to San Francisco to see what the situation was Stateside. George reported that '… the attorney handling the sale had died' and that a deal could be done, but that he would have to act fast to meet American time-zone 'deadlines' and added that he '… could make arrangements to return the locomotive home'. George was asked that if the finance was arranged and *Flying Scotsman* was returned home, would he '… be willing to run the locomotive in Britain?' George said 'Yes!' and so a deal was done.

So Bill McAlpine payed for No.4472 to be returned to the UK via the Panama Canal in February 1973 and as it was in such good condition, the BR authorities allowed *Flying Scotsman* to run with its two tenders under its own steam from Liverpool to Derby Works. At Derby, the Californian sun-scorched paintwork of *Flying Scotsman* was removed and No.4472's paintwork was restored to its former glory. It became the first LNER apple green livery that Derby had ever applied.

After Derby, No.4472 moved to the Paignton and Dartmouth Steam Railway in the summer of 1973. It was then transferred to Market Overton in Lincolnshire, where No.4472 kept company with her nemesis from Wembley in 1925, No.4079, *Pendennis Castle*, also owned by Bill McAlpine.

Waved on by thousands of people who lined the trackside, *Flying Scotsman* ran light engine – that's under its own power – from Edge Hill, Liverpool, to Derby Works. *Flying Scotsman* is seen having arrived at Derby Station and is just about to manoeuvre into the works for attention. (Sir William McAlpine Collection)

After its return from North America, *Flying Scotsman* stood outside Derby Works from 19 February 1973 until 14 July, awaiting attention. The damage caused by the Californian sun to *Flying Scotsman*'s paintwork is seen to good effect in this image. (Sir William McAlpine Collection)

No.4472 *Flying Scotsman* is seen working an enthusiasts charter 'The Son of Skirl', at Lostock Junction on 20 September 1987. (Sir William McAlpine Collection)

Flying Scotsman was then transferred to Steamtown, Carnforth, from where it worked various rail tours around the country.

In 1986, Bill McAlpine decided to lease a two-road former diesel maintenance shop at Southall depot and this became the new base for No.4472 until 2004.

During the autumn of 1987, a suggestion came from the National Railway Museum (NRM) to Bill McAlpine, saying that, 'as they' – the NRM – '... were unable to release "World Speed Record Holder" *Mallard*, for shipment to Australia, for the Bi-Centennial Celebrations, perhaps they' – the NRM – '... could suggest that Bill McAlpine was interested in sending No.4472 *Flying Scotsman* instead ...'

Walter Stutchbery and his Aus Steam '88 colleagues burned the midnight oil in discussion, raised the finance and finally agreed the complete package for the visit with Bill's people in England. When asked how he felt about *Flying Scotsman* going to Australia, and bearing in mind what happened when *Scotsman* went to the US, Bill said that he '... was very excited indeed at the thought of taking *Flying Scotsman* to the other side of the world! And that [they] had learned from previous lessons and

had in place the money to bring her home before she left the country!'

In October 1988, *Flying Scotsman* arrived in Australia to take part in the country's bicentenary celebrations as a central attraction in the Aus Steam '88 festival, where it travelled more than

▲ No.4472 *Flying Scotsman* is seen passing Burradoo, New South Wales, on 19 October 1988, on its delivery run from Sydney to Melbourne. (Rob Turner)

28,000 miles over Australian rails, including a transcontinental run from Sydney to Perth.

On 8 August 1989, *Flying Scotsman* set a world record for the longest non-stop run for steam traction. The locomotive ran from Parkes to Broken Hill in Australia – a distance of 422 miles, 7.59 chains, in 9 hours 25 minutes with 535 tons gross. Seven British and Australian drivers were used, as were three 10,000-gallon water gins.

In September 1989, *Flying Scotsman* travelled to the very extremities of Western Australia – Perth. On one occasion very reminiscent of the days of the Wild West, *Flying Scotsman* met with its nemesis from

◄ *Flying Scotsman* is seen in the railway yard at Moss Vale in the Southern Highlands of New South Wales on 12 January 1989. (Rob Turner)

the 1925 Wembley Exhibition, *Pendennis Castle*, 'smokebox to smokebox'! *Flying Scotsman*'s adventures in Australia turned out to be an extended tour lasting some fifteen months before it arrived back at Tilbury Docks in December 1989. No.4472 *Flying Scotsman* had safely returned home.

On 2 May 1990, complete with the commemorative headboard that it had carried on its world record-breaking non-stop run to Alice Springs, No.4472 *Flying Scotsman* made its first main-line run on BR tracks following its return from Australia. The route was from Paddington to Banbury, where it stopped for water and then travelled to Carnforth via Acocks Green. From Carnforth, it then worked a

► On 11 March 1989, two trains ran from Sydney to Moss Vale and return. One train was hauled by 4-6-2 class 38 locomotive No.3801; the other was worked by No.4472 *Flying Scotsman*. The more generous Australian loading gauge may be noted with the two locomotives seen side by side at Moss Vale. (Rob Turner)

series of tours including some 'Cumbrian Coast Express' charter specials.

From April to July 1993, No.4472 *Flying Scotsman* was at Babcock, Robey Ltd Works for a heavy repair. Sir William had already made it known that he was happy for the volunteers to have the loco painted in a colour of their own choice as a 'thank you present' for their help with running the locomotive. Babcock's Managing Director

Here is the headboard that was carried on the front of *Flying Scotsman* during its amazing trip from Melbourne to Alice Springs and return. It is seen displayed on the wall of Southall depot's workshop, but has since been moved to the workshops of Sir William McAlpine, at his Fawley Hill Railway Centre. (Author)

No.4472 *Flying Scotsman* pausing at Exeter – not in Devon, England, but in the Southern Highlands of New South Wales, Australia – on 18 December 1988, during its return journey from Melbourne to Sydney. (Rob Turner)

spoke to Roland Kennington, the chief engineer of *Flying Scotsman*, and said that '... when the overhaul was completed he wanted something really spectacular to finish the overhaul off and so create much publicity'. Roland had for some time wanted to retro-fit a double chimney, German-style smoke deflectors, and paint the locomotive in BR green livery. When the Managing Director heard about this, he was absolutely

On 19 August 1989, at a place just south of Alice Springs, a brief parallel run took place with No.4472 *Flying Scotsman* and a 4-8-2 steam locomotive, No.124, of the recently restored 3ft 6in gauge 'Old Ghan' line, which originally ran from Port Augusta. (Sir William McAlpine Collection)

The words on the plate say it all. (Roland Kennington)

delighted and offered to pay for a new smokebox, double chimney and smoke deflectors to be fitted. The locomotive was duly out-shopped in BR dark green livery and its running number was changed to No.60103, the number it had carried at the end of its BR career. In this form, *Flying Scotsman* received much acclaim among enthusiasts and the public alike.

On 25 July 1993, No.60103 *Flying Scotsman* recommenced its tour of preserved railways starting with its second visit to the Paignton and Dartmouth Railway. Then, in September 1993, No.60103 visited the Gloucester and Warwickshire Railway.

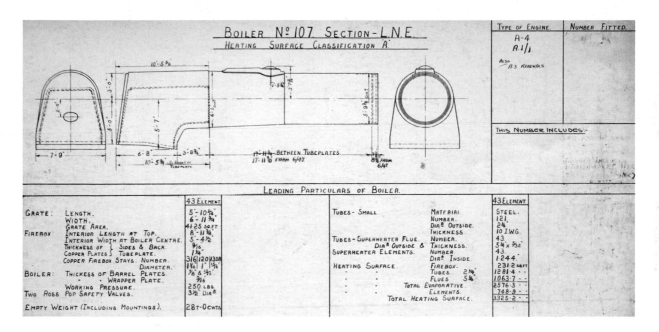

BOILER N⁰ 107. SECTION – L.N.E.
HEATING SURFACE CLASSIFICATION "A"

TYPE OF ENGINE.	NUMBER FITTED.
A-4 A.1/1	
ALSO A.3 RENEWALS	

THIS NUMBER INCLUDES:-

LEADING PARTICULARS OF BOILER.

		43 ELEMENT				43 ELEMENT
GRATE:	LENGTH.	5'-10⅜"	TUBES - SMALL	MATERIAL	STEEL.	
	WIDTH.	6'-11¾"		NUMBER.	121.	
	GRATE AREA.	41.25 SQ.FT.		DIA⁰ OUTSIDE.	2¼	
FIREBOX	INTERIOR LENGTH AT TOP.	8'-11¾"		THICKNESS.	10 I.W.G.	
	INTERIOR WIDTH AT BOILER CENTRE.	5'-4½"	TUBES - SUPERHEATER FLUE.	NUMBER.	43.	
	THICKNESS OF } SIDES & BACK.	9/16	DIA⁰ OUTSIDE &	THICKNESS.	5¼ x 9/32	
	COPPER PLATES } TUBEPLATE.	1¼	SUPERHEATER ELEMENTS.	NUMBER.	43.	
	COPPER FIREBOX STAYS. NUMBER.	316 120 1308		DIA² INSIDE.	1.244.	
	DIAMETER.	1¹⁶/₁₆ 1" 1¹⁵/₁₆	HEATING SURFACE.	FIREBOX.	231.2 SQFT	
BOILER:	THICKNESS OF BARREL PLATES.	⅞ & ¹³/₁₆	" "	TUBES. 2¼	1281.4 · ·	
	" WRAPPER PLATE.	9/16	" "	FLUES. 5¼	1063.7 · ·	
	WORKING PRESSURE.	250 LBS	" " TOTAL EVAPORATIVE.		2576.3 · ·	
TWO ROSS POP SAFETY VALVES.		3½ DIA⁰	" "	ELEMENTS.	748.9 · ·	
			TOTAL HEATING SURFACE.		3325.2 · ·	
EMPTY WEIGHT (INCLUDING MOUNTINGS).		28T-0CWTS.				

▲ Between 16 December 1977 and 6 June 1978, No.4472 *Flying Scotsman* was in the works of Vickers at Barrow-in-Furness for a heavy repair. Its boiler, No.27020, previously fitted to No.60041 *Salmon Trout*, was replaced with boiler No.27971, built to diagram No.107 and which was new in October 1960. This was a boiler type normally associated with A4 class locomotives, previously having been fitted to A4 class 4-6-2 No.60019 *Bittern* and becoming the seventeenth boiler that *Flying Scotsman* had carried. The diagram shows the general arrangement of a boiler of type No.107 design, as fitted to *Flying Scotsman* from June 1978 until its overhaul at the NRM, after which this boiler was sold. The type No.107 boilers were fitted generally to the A3 class locomotives as standard when the earlier boilers of type No.94 required replacement. (Peter Townend Collection)

As *Flying Scotsman* continued touring preserved railways, Bill McAlpine (now Sir William), decided to sell *Flying Scotsman* to pay off a mortgage on the locomotive. Pete Waterman approached Sir William and offered to merge his railway interests with those of Sir William's. So on 21 September 1993 '*Flying Scotsman* Enterprises' and 'Waterman Railways' merged to form '*Flying Scotsman* Railways'. Although Sir William and Pete both owned the new company between them, it was agreed that Pete would run the business side of the new company.

All was going well with *Flying Scotsman*'s 'Grand Tour' of private preserved railways around the country, until disaster struck when working on the Llangollen Railway. On 22 April 1995, *Flying Scotsman* was derailed during an empty stock movement with 'all wheels' of the locomotive

coming off the track before it came to rest. *Flying Scotsman* was re-railed but, as boiler pressure was being raised, steam was seen escaping at about head height from the 'back-head' of the boiler into the cab. The crack was deemed to have been hastened by the derailment. *Flying Scotsman* was deemed a total failure by the

Pete Waterman, on the left, was a 50 per cent owner of *Flying Scotsman* with Sir William McAlpine during the 1990s. He is in the cab of *Flying Scotsman* with Roland Kennington, chief engineer, during the A3's visit to the Swanage Railway during September 1964. (Andrew P.M. Wright)

Did You Know?

Flying Scotsman received the most expensive and extensive overhaul ever carried out to a steam locomotive in private ownership? On the 23rd February 1996 in a handshake worth £1,500,000, *Flying Scotsman*, was bought by Dr Tony Marchington and the next major overhaul of *Flying Scotsman* was resumed in earnest. Between 1996 and 1999 it was restored to running condition at a further cost of £1 million, and became the most extensive and expensive overhaul ever carried out to a steam locomotive owned privately.

▲ *Flying Scotsman* runs around its train at Swanage during a visit there in 1994. (Author)

boiler insurance company and immediately withdrawn from service. The distance run on nine preserved railways since October 1992 was approximately 30,500 miles.

On 6 June 1995, *Flying Scotsman* returned to Southall, where the dismantling process was started in preparation for its next major overhaul.

Did You Know?

Flying Scotsman appeared in the Disney film *102 Dalmatians* in 2000.

Glenn Close stars as Cruella de Vil in the sequel to the 1961 film *101 Dalmatians*. Cruella attempts to steal puppies for her 'grandest' fur coat yet and *Flying Scotsman* is seen pulling the 'Orient Express' Pullman train out of St Pancras Station in a shot which lasts just 5 seconds!

Flying Scotsman continued its tour of private railways by being moved by road to the Paignton & Dartmouth Railway, where it completed 2,730 miles. The locomotive is seen crossing Churston Viaduct with a passenger service. (D. Trevor Rowe)

An idyllic view of No.60103 *Flying Scotsman* on the Nene Valley Railway in the 1990s. (D. Trevor Rowe)

On 28 May 1995, ultrasonic tests were carried out on two areas of *Flying Scotsman*'s boiler, which showed extensive cracking on the 'water side' of the right-hand side plate accompanied by grooving to a depth of 3–4mm in plates which were 12mm thick. The crack, which was visible for a distance of 3¼in, extended on the internal surfaces a further 8in in the other direction, making a total crack length of 17in. On the downward side this crack ran out into a groove which varied in length from 3–4mm for a further distance of 11mm. After a further 6in there was a further groove 5in long. Lower down, at a point 28in above the footplate, there was an internal crack which extended for a further 6in. These findings were unacceptable to the engineering surveyor and in view of this no further remedial work was carried out. (Roland Kennington)

Did You Know?

Upon completion of the filming of *102 Dalmatians*, *Flying Scotsman* became the last steam locomotive to depart from St Pancras Station, before the station was reconstructed as the London Terminal of Eurostar services to Continental Europe via High Speed 1 and the Channel Tunnel.

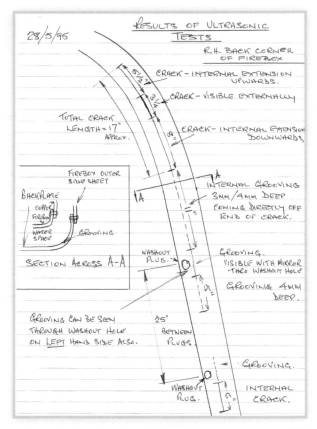

28/5/95

RESULTS OF ULTRASONIC TESTS

R.H. BACK CORNER OF FIREBOX

CRACK – INTERNAL EXTENSION UPWARDS.

CRACK – VISIBLE EXTERNALLY

TOTAL CRACK LENGTH = 17" APPROX.

CRACK – INTERNAL EXTENSION DOWNWARDS.

FIREBOX OUTER SIDE SHEET

BACKPLATE

CORNER FIREBOX

WATER SPACE

GROOVING

SECTION ACROSS A–A

INTERNAL GROOVING 3MM/4MM DEEP COMING DIRECTLY OFF END OF CRACK.

WASHOUT PLUG.

GROOVING. VISIBLE WITH MIRROR THRO WASHOUT HOLE

GROOVING 4MM DEEP.

GROOVING CAN BE SEEN THROUGH WASHOUT HOLE ON LEFT HAND SIDE ALSO.

25" BETWEEN PLUGS.

GROOVING.

WASHOUT PLUG.

INTERNAL CRACK.

▲ After its tour of preserved railways, No.60103 *Flying Scotsman* arrived back at its home depot at Southall on 9 June 1995. On 22 June, dismantling was authorised in preparation for its next major overhaul. No.60103 is seen inside its home depot shed just prior to dismantling beginning. (Fred Stenle)

Salvation for *Flying Scotsman* came a third time, when Dr Tony Marchington bought the locomotive and had it restored over three years to main-line running condition. Tony was the man who owned the ultimate in big boys' toys – a magnificent collection of traction engines and fairground equipment – and there was little more left to relish. But Tony was a person who very much enjoyed life, Freemasonry and his family.

Tony then went on to buy the A4 class Pacific No.60019 *Bittern*, so that there was another locomotive available to run excursions when *Flying Scotsman* was being serviced – well, that was the theory. This made him the only individual to personally own two Gresley Pacific locomotives.

After a three-year rebuild, *Flying Scotsman* worked 'The Inaugural Scotsman' charter train from King's Cross to York on 4 July 1999. With the world's media recording the event and thousands of well-wishers lining the track side to observe the passing of a legend, Tony then authorised the running of excursion trips around the country.

During 2002, as *Flying Scotsman* saw regular use on the VSOE British Pullman trains, investors seeking their own bit of

Did You Know?
Due to excessively high running costs, *Flying Scotsman* was put up for sale and after a successful campaign in 2004, it was returned to public ownership and was bought by the NRM for £2.3 million.

During June 1995 dismantling began for the next major overhaul of *Flying Scotsman*. With the external plate work removed, it's seen here having the boiler insulation (consisting of rock wool) removed by some of *Flying Scotsman*'s volunteer team. (Fred Stenle)

In this view, the refurbishment of *Flying Scotsman* has advanced to such an extent that the 'bottom end' is all but complete. The next job would be the fitting of the boiler. (Fred Stenle)

In this view the buffer beam has been stripped back to base metal, with the exception of 'A3', which signifies *Flying Scotsman*'s class. A closer look will show the rivet heads holding the buffer beam to the various sections of the frames. (Author)

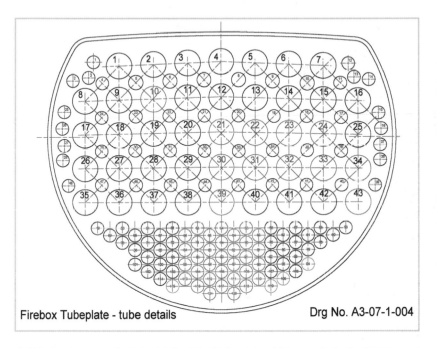

Firebox Tubeplate - tube details

Drg No. A3-07-1-004

▲ This drawing shows the tube details of the 'firebox tube plate' as per boiler No.27971, which had previously been fitted to A4 class 4-6-2 No.60019 *Bittern*. Boiler No.27971 was originally carried by *Flying Scotsman* from 16 June 1978 and was refitted during its overhaul during the Dr Tony Marchington era. (Roland Kennington)

During June 1999, *Flying Scotsman* went through a period of commissioning after its £1 million overhaul. Testing included static steaming tests and short runs up and down Southall yard within the limits of the depot. With the locomotive in steam for eighty hours or so, some 10 miles were covered during this period. Here its tender is being replenished and *Flying Scotsman*, in undercoat grey, waits for further testing in Southall yard. (Fred Stenle)

And you thought that the mechanics of a steam locomotive were simple! Dated 1 December 1998, here is a revised version of a schematic diagram of the 'Air Braking System' for *Flying Scotsman*, as was used during the Dr Tony Marchington era. (Roland Kennington)

railway history were given a chance to 'get on board' after *Flying Scotsman*'s directors announced that they were extending the deadline for applications for shares in this £2 million flotation. Indeed, more than 1,000 *Flying Scotsman* fans bought shares, raising £850,000. The amount of cash raised meant that the company then had an extra £1.95 million at its disposal, as on the completion of the share issue, £1.1 million of debt was converted into equity.

With *Flying Scotsman* plc joining the OFEX exchange for smaller firms in March, it was planned to turn the loco into a profitable business and the company was valued at around £4.7 million. But in September 2002, the *Edinburgh Evening News* stated that in its first set of interim

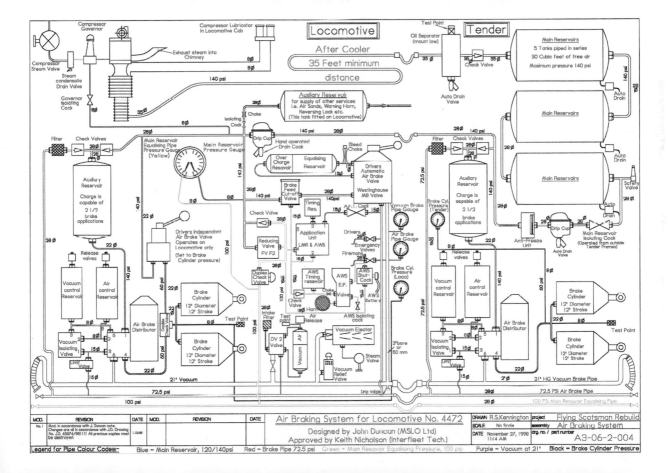

Locomotive — **Tender**

Air Braking System for Locomotive No. 4472

Designed by John Duncan (MSLO Ltd)
Approved by Keith Nicholson (Interfleet Tech.)

DRAWN R.S.Kennington — project Flying Scotsman Rebuild
SCALE No Scale — assembly Air Braking System
DATE November 27, 1998 11:14 AM — drg. no. / part number A3-06-2-004

Legend for Pipe Colour Codes:- Blue = Main Reservoir, 120/140psi Red = Brake Pipe 72.5 psi Green = Main Resevoir Equalising Pressure, 100 psi Purple = Vacuum at 21" Block = Brake Cylinder Pressure

Did You Know?

The image of *Flying Scotsman* is depicted on the specially produced £5 coin as a tribute to Britain's industrialisation. These coins were struck to celebrate pride in Britain's heritage and to commemorate the London 2012 Olympic Games. This was part of the 'Celebration of Britain' series of £5 sterling silver coins with eighteen different coins making a complete set. These coins had a limited issue of 95,000.

➤ Beautifully burnished and ready to be fitted on the boiler of *Flying Scotsman* is one of its works plates. It is made of brass – looks like pure gold, but to some it's priceless. (Author)

results since flotation, *Flying Scotsman* plc posted a pre-tax loss of £276,000 for the six months to the end of June, compared with a £320,000 deficit for the same period the previous year.

Then in late 2003, Dr Tony Marchington was declared bankrupt and consequently was required to sell off his collection of traction engines and fairground rides. At the company's AGM in October 2003, CEO Peter Butler announced losses of £474,619 and with a £1.5 million overdraft at Barclays Bank, stated that the company only had enough cash to trade until April 2004. After the company failed to declare interim results, the company's shares were suspended from OFEX on 3 November 2003.

In February 2004 it was announced that a vintage car dealer had been drafted in to seek potential buyers for the historic locomotive, with a guide price of £2.5 million believed to have been suggested.

Did You Know?

Flying Scotsman is the subject of continuing debate as to which colour it should be painted. In forty years of continuous revenue-earning service, it underwent several changes to its livery. Alan Pegler's preferred option was to return the locomotive as far as possible to the general appearance and distinctive colour it carried at the height of its fame in the 1930s (this version of livery was also carried during the McAlpine era). During the Marchington era, it was running in a hybrid form, retaining the modernised exhaust arrangements while carrying the LNER apple green livery of the 1930s. Some believe that the more famous LNER colour scheme should remain, while others take the view that, to be authentic, only BR livery should be used when the locomotive is carrying these later additions as per BR running, but while in BR livery it never ran with a corridor tender. In February 2011, the NRM announced that *Flying Scotsman* would be painted in LNER wartime black livery, with the letters 'NE' on the sides of the tender, along with the number 103 on one side of the cab and 502 on the other – the numbers it was given under the LNER's renumbering system during the war. The NRM then said that *Flying Scotsman* would be repainted in its familiar apple green livery after testing and commissioning tests were completed, but with a double Kylchap blast-pipe and chimney and with German-style smoke deflectors. However, what is certain is that whichever colour it is painted, there will always be someone objecting for one reason or another.

◄ No.4472 *Flying Scotsman* works the 'Inaugural Scotsman' special charter from King's Cross to York, through Finsbury Park Station on 4 July 1999. (Author)

◄ In magnificent condition both mechanically and externally, No.4472 *Flying Scotsman* is seen working one of its first enthusiasts special workings after the most expensive and extensive overhaul ever carried out to a steam locomotive in private ownership. (Author's Collection)

► No.4472 *Flying Scotsman* waits for the right of way at Slough during an excursion from Paddington during 1999. There is more than enough steam to spare; this phenomenon seems to occur more in the preservation era and is due to the inexperience of the crew. (Grahame Plater)

Geoff Courtney, spokesman for *Flying Scotsman*, said that '… the chance of the locomotive being sold abroad was absolutely minimal because of its importance to Britain', but refused to comment on claims that the sale move had been prompted by fears that a major bank might seize and auction the locomotive to recoup debts.

Flying Scotsman plc directors then decided to put its prize asset up for sale and asked international property advisers GVA Grimley to hold a sealed bidding process, effectively auctioning the legendary locomotive.

The outcome of the sale was announced on 5 April, when it was revealed that the National Railway Museum had been successful in their bid to buy *Flying Scotsman*. Because of the general public's active interest in saving *Flying Scotsman*, it became known as 'the people's engine'.

On 16 October 2011, Dr Tony Marchington died of cancer aged 56.

No.4472 *Flying Scotsman* is ready to depart yet again in the Marchington era at King's Cross Station. It's fitted with German-style smoke deflectors, which, although historically incorrect as they were not carried by *Flying Scotsman* when it originally carried apple green livery, certainly helped improve the driver's vision as it was fitted with a double chimney which caused a softer exhaust. (Author's Collection)

No.4472 *Flying Scotsman* is waiting to depart from Platform 2 at Victoria Station, London, with a VSOE British Pullman train working during 2002. (Frank Hornby)

No.4472 *Flying Scotsman* stands at Stewarts Lane depot with its smoke box door open, revealing a sight not normally seen by the general public: the ashes and dust left over from the burned coal of a previous run. This debris will need to be removed before the fire is lit once more and is part of the preparations needed for *Flying Scotsman*'s next outing. (Fred Stenle)

The year 2003 marked the 150th anniversary of the opening of the Great Northern Railway's works at Doncaster. To mark this occasion an open weekend was organised for railway enthusiasts. *Flying Scotsman* is seen there on 25 July 2003, the day before the event formally opened. (Derek Crunkhorn)

Over 250 friends and family attended his funeral at St James' church, Buxworth on 28 October 2011.

Tony had bought *Flying Scotsman* at a cost of £1.5 million and after a three-year restoration costing a further £1 million, No.4472 *Flying Scotsman* returned to working on the main line in 1999. When it was sold to the NRM in 2004, it was in better condition than when he had bought it in 1996.

No.4472, *Flying Scotsman*, appeared at the NRM's Railfest event between 29 May and 6 June 2004. It then ran for some twelve months, with interim running repairs, to raise funds for its ten-year major boiler recertification. But in 2005, when No.4472 *Flying Scotsman* was scheduled to work one of the NRM's York to Scarborough steam excursions, due to a problem with a superheater element, it was withdrawn from service and work was scheduled to repair it as soon as possible. Duly repaired, it returned to service and worked many specials around the country, including 'Christmas Lunch' specials from Dorridge to Leicester.

Did You Know?

Flying Scotsman has undergone eighteen boiler changes since it was completed in 1923. As was normal railway practice, every few years a locomotive would be sent to the works to have a mechanical overhaul carried out. During this period it would have its boiler replaced with a refurbished one, so saving time of it being out of traffic. Also, as techniques improved, new features would be incorporated into the boiler's design. Locomotives therefore would carry many different boilers during the course of their lifetime in service. To date, *Flying Scotsman* has carried a total of nineteen different boilers.

Then in January 2006 an NRM Press Release stated that: 'No.4472 *Flying Scotsman* had entered the NRM's workshops for its major mainline overhaul.' Within a short time *Flying Scotsman* was rapidly dismantled. During the dismantling process, it was confirmed that the right-hand cylinder had a crack from 'end to end', but the NRM did have a spare.

During its overhaul, it was decided to revert to using the A3 class pattern boiler, which was currently the spare. Its then current A4-type boiler, which was used on No.4472 during its last period in steam, was sold to raise funds for *Flying Scotsman*'s overhaul.

Over the following years the remedial work continued and with the NRM's overhaul of *Flying Scotsman* finally coming to an end during the summer of 2011 – or so it was thought – *Flying Scotsman* was again fitted with a double chimney and unveiled

to a specially selected group of dignitaries on 27 May 2011. *Flying Scotsman* was then sent to Bury to be 'finished off'. However, new cracks were found in the frames and the locomotive had to be stripped down once more for more remedial work. Was this protracted overhaul started in 2006 ever going to finish?

On 27 May 2004, No.4472 *Flying Scotsman* with its support coach, No.17013, worked the first leg of its transfer from Southall to the NRM at York. *Flying Scotsman* is seen at Tyseley depot, replenishing its water before continuing to Derby for the next scheduled stop. (Author)

◀ *Flying Scotsman* is seen waiting to depart from York with the 'Scarborough Spa Express' in 2004, shortly after it had become part of the National Railway Museum's collection. (Adrian Scales)

▲ A classic railway scene with a classic locomotive, as No.4472 *Flying Scotsman* departs from Scarborough Station during 2004. A spate of failures with No.4472 had necessitated including the NRM-owned former royal train locomotive No.47798 *Prince William* in the formation. This was so it could rescue the train should No.4472 fail unexpectedly and it's seen immediately behind the tender. (Adrian Scales)

By the end of October 2012, the work being undertaken included the fitting of a newly manufactured bogie stretcher, the overhauling of bogie components, the manufacture and fitting of ash-pan components, the manufacture and fitting of the cab floor, and the overhaul and fitting of the lubrication system. There was still no end date in sight for *Flying Scotsman* to steam again in the foreseeable future.

On 26 October 2012, the NRM's report on *Flying Scotsman* was published. The report started: '*Flying Scotsman* began a major overhaul in January 2006 that was scheduled to last one year and cost around £750,000. In October 2012, the cost of the overhaul had risen to around £2.7 million and hadn't been completed.' It continued, '... the purchase of *Flying Scotsman* by the NRM would always have gone ahead, regardless of the locomotive's actual condition, given the aspiration to

Did You Know?
Flying Scotsman has been associated with nine different tenders of five different designs. The first was a GNR-designed 8-wheeled tender and ran with *Flying Scotsman* from new. The second was a GNR-designed 6-wheeled tender normally paired with a K3 class locomotive, but due to insufficient room at the British Empire Exhibition at Wembley in 1925, this tender was substituted until 16 November 1925.

The boiler 'back-head' from *Flying Scotsman* is seen at the workshops of Riley & Son (E) Ltd during the spring of 2012. Once the boiler had been lowered onto the frames, then the cab would be replaced. (Author)

save it on behalf of the nation. The NRM acquired the locomotive in a "sealed-bid" auction, where there was no opportunity to negotiate on price.'

In January 2013 the restoration of *Flying Scotsman* moved into its eighth year, with the revelation of yet another serious mechanical flaw. This was the discovery that 'the middle cylinder was mis-aligned by as much as an inch and that the locomotive may have to

The number 103 is seen painted on the cab of *Flying Scotsman* at the works of Riley & Son (E) Ltd, Bury, in 2012. *Flying Scotsman* originally carried the number 103 and wartime black livery between May 1946 and January 1947. (Author)

be stripped down for a fourth time'. *Flying Scotsman* was at this time already more than five years late on delivery after its overhaul and had a budget overspend of £3 million.

So with no obvious end date in sight for its overhaul, whenever *Flying Scotsman* is finished, it will undoubtedly be pulling in the crowds of admirers for many years to come. It's not called 'the most famous steam locomotive in the world' for nothing!

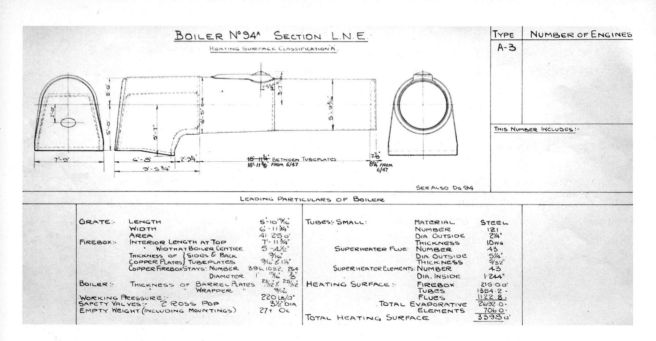

BOILER Nº 94ᴬ SECTION L.N.E.

HEATING SURFACE CLASSIFICATION 'A'.

TYPE	NUMBER OF ENGINES
A-3	
	THIS NUMBER INCLUDES:-

SEE ALSO DG 94

8'-0"

2'-6"

5'-0"

5'-7"

5'-5¼"

5'-9½"

5-5⅜"

15-7"

7'-0"

6'-8" 2'-9½"

3'-5¾"

18'-11½" BETWEEN TUBEPLATES
18'-11⅝" FROM 6/47

7⅞"

8¼" FROM 6/47

LEADING PARTICULARS OF BOILER

GRATE:-	LENGTH	5'-10⅞"	
	WIDTH	6'-11¾"	
	AREA	41.25 ☐'	
FIREBOX:-	INTERIOR LENGTH AT TOP	7'-11¾"	
	WIDTH AT BOILER CENTRE	5-4½"	
	THICKNESS OF ⎰ SIDES & BACK	9/16"	
	(COPPER PLATES) ⎱ TUBEPLATES	9/16 & 1¼"	
	COPPER FIREBOX STAYS: NUMBER	396,1052, 864	
	DIAMETER	1" 15/16" ⅞"	
BOILER:-	THICKNESS OF BARREL PLATES	23/32 & 25/32	
	WRAPPER "	9/16"	
WORKING PRESSURE:-		220 LB/☐'	
SAFETY VALVES:- 2 ROSS POP		3½" DIA	
EMPTY WEIGHT (INCLUDING MOUNTINGS)		27T 0C	

TUBES:- SMALL:-	MATERIAL	STEEL
	NUMBER	121
	DIA OUTSIDE	2¼"
	THICKNESS	10 WG
SUPERHEATER FLUE: NUMBER		43
	DIA OUTSIDE	5¼"
	THICKNESS	5/32"
SUPERHEATER ELEMENTS: NUMBER		43
	DIA. INSIDE	1.244"
HEATING SURFACE :-	FIREBOX	215·0 ☐'
	TUBES	1354·2 ·
	FLUES	1122.8 ·
TOTAL EVAPORATIVE		2692·0·
	ELEMENTS	706·0·
TOTAL HEATING SURFACE		3398 ☐'

▲ During *Flying Scotsman*'s protracted overhaul by the NRM, the decision was made to remove boiler No.27971 of diagram No.107, which had earlier been fitted to A4 class 4-6-2 No.60019 *Bittern*. This had been carried by *Flying Scotsman* from 6 June 1978. A spare boiler, No.27020 of type 94A, was overhauled to replace it. The diagram shows the type of boiler currently fitted to *Flying Scotsman*. (Peter Townend Collection)

ecause of the LNER's emphasis on using *Flying Scotsman* for publicity purposes and then its ever-continuing antics in preservation – including two international forays – *Flying Scotsman* is surely without doubt 'the most famous steam locomotive in the world' today.

Alan Pegler saved *Flying Scotsman* and early in 1973, Sir William McAlpine took over that responsibility and took the locomotive to Australia, where it broke yet another record – the longest non-stop run for a steam locomotive at 442 miles. Then with Pete Waterman having a hand in running *Flying Scotsman* in the 1990s, that responsibility then passed on to Dr Tony Marchington in 1996, when it broke another record by having the most expensive and extensive overhaul ever carried out to a steam locomotive. On again it moved, this

➤ In April 1929, No.4472 *Flying Scotsman* starred in the first sound feature film to be produced in England – *The Flying Scotsman* – which is also famous for some very daring stunt work done on the train itself. Here *Flying Scotsman* is being filmed by the film company, who mounted a camera on a flat wagon which was propelled by another steam locomotive. (Author's Collection)

time to the National Railway Museum in 2004, where, under its ownership, it again broke world records for the cost of its protracted overhaul.

Who knows what further world records it will break and what exciting adventures await *Flying Scotsman* in the years to come?

Mantled by snow after a rough transatlantic crossing, No.4472 *Flying Scotsman* was unloaded from the deck of the container vessel *California Star* by the floating crane *Mammoth* on 14 February 1973. The return journey to Liverpool had been via the Panama Canal. (Sir William McAlpine Collection)

▲ Given works number 1564, the first express passenger locomotive to be completed and make its debut for the newly formed London & North Eastern Railway left Doncaster Works on 7 February 1923, having cost £7,944 to construct. Almost fifty years to the day, on 17 February 1983, that very same locomotive is seen on the turntable at Carnforth. (David Ward Collection)

▲ On the non-stop 'Flying Scotsman' runs between King's Cross and Edinburgh Waverley, the footplate crews would change over at Tollerton, 10 miles north of York, and this was effected through the corridor tender. Here we see at close quarters part of the detail of the end of the corridor tender attached to No.4472 *Flying Scotsman* during the McAlpine era. (David Ward Collection)

No.4472 *Flying Scotsman* is seen working the 'Cumbrian Mountain Express' during the early 1980s. (David Ward Collection)

'A Rake Of Railwaymen'. Each of the people in this photograph played a major role in the running of *Flying Scotsman*. From the right is Alan Bloom smoking his pipe; he approached Bill McAlpine to arrange a rescue mission to repatriate *Flying Scotsman* from California. Next is David Ward driving the locomotive; he was the Director of Special Trains for BR (1986–94), and operations director for *Flying Scotsman* (1996–2004). Next is Alan Pegler, who bought *Flying Scotsman* in 1963. Next is the back of Alan's wife and on the far left is George Hinchcliffe, who was No.4472's manager; when the US tour became a financial disaster he became the tour manager in North America. He also negotiated a deal for *Flying Scotsman* to be shipped home, with Bill McAlpine financing the operation. Finally, at George's side, is his son Richard, who went with *Flying Scotsman* on its North American tour. They are all enjoying a ride on No.25, a former Beckton Gas Works 0-4-0 locomotive, at Bressingham Gardens Railway. (David Ward Collection)

In BR green livery, *Flying Scotsman* is seen working a demonstration 'Talisman' service on the Nene Valley Railway during the summer of 1994. (D. Trevor Rowe)

Here are three of *Flying Scotsman*'s owners at an event at the National Railway Museum. On the left is Alan Pegler OBE, owner 1963–72; next is Dr Tony Marchington, owner 1996–2004 and Sir William McAlpine Bt, owner 1973–96. (Sir William McAlpine Collection)

Flying Scotsman is seen in wartime black livery at the NRM's 2012 Railfest event. (Author)